Taking the Word to Heart

Five Ways to Get a Grip on God's Word

Endorsements for Taking the Word to Heart

"Internalizing God's Word is our source of strength as Christ's disciples. All too often, our generation has substituted spiritual feelings for the godly thoughts and actions that are encouraged by the discipline of Scripture memory. Nancy Taylor's highly motivational authorship weaves Biblical truth and spiritual application together in a way that inspires the desire for spiritual maturity. May the refreshing message of this much needed book be a blessing to many."

Billie Hanks, Jr.
President, International Evangelism Association

"Without a doubt, scripture memory is the heartbeat of Nancy Taylor. It is God's Word that sustains, motivates and captivates us. Nancy does a tremendous job giving the "nuts and bolts" along with the inspiration to place God's Word in our hearts. You can trust this book to challenge and lead you closer to the Lord."

Gregg Matte
Senior Pastor, Houston's First Baptist Church

"The longer I walk with Christ and help others do the same, the more convinced I am of how critical it is that I hide God's Word in my heart (Psalm 119:11). As I 'meditate on it day and night' (Joshua 1:8), its impact on my own life and transformation is unparalleled. Nancy's book *Taking the Word to Heart* has helped not only me but those I disciple to better make this a reality. This book encourages, equips, and empowers disciples and disciplemakers to make Scripture memory a practical part of our Christian walk."

Margaret Fitzwater
Co-Director, Navigator Church Ministries, The Navigators

"*Taking The Word To Heart* is a passionate appeal for all believers to deeply embrace and treasure God's eternal Word. The cry of the author to memorize, meditate upon and be transformed by God's Word flows out of an authentic lifestyle. I was moved by how the author does not speak from theory, but from a life that has become permeated by God's wisdom. The book provides very practical advice for making God's Word a part of everyday life and ministry. Recent research shows that most Christians do not memorize and meditate upon the Bible. The Body of Christ can be greatly strengthened by embracing the challenge of *Taking The Word To Heart*."

Brad J. Waggoner
Broadman and Holman Publishing Group

"*Taking The Word To Heart* is a joy to read and a treasure to hide deep in one's life. The book is intensely practical and easy to use. I found its combination of spiritual tools and personal illustrations well balanced. Pass it on!"

Waylon B. Moore
Founder and President of Missions Unlimited

"Nancy Taylor loves the Word of God! The Word comes alive when she speaks. Whether Nancy speaks the Word over you individually, or has spoken the Word over an event you are attending, your heart will be changed and peace will cover you.

Taking the Word to Heart will not only deepen your love for God's Word, it will cause you to hunger to know more of it and will equip you to effectively memorize it and confidently speak it."

Carolyn O'Neal
Director of Women's Ministry
Houston's First Baptist Church

"In *Taking the Word to Heart* Nancy does an amazing job of inviting you to taste and experience the transforming power of God's Word. There is nothing more important than memorizing and meditating on Scripture, and this is, by far, the best and most practical book on the subject I have ever read.

I've known Nancy for several decades and Scripture permeates her heart. She is an anointed, humble woman of God, and in this book you will discover her secret. Your hunger and thirst for the Word of God will be revitalized!

As Nancy so masterfully illustrates, Scripture memory will: dramatically enhance your walk with God, help guide you in daily decisions, and completely alter your outlook on life. You will finally be able to experience the victorious Christian life you have always longed for and you will be "marked" and forever changed!"

Billy Beacham
Founder and President of Student Discipleship Ministries
See You at the Pole

Taking the Word to Heart

Five Ways to Get a Grip on God's Word

Nancy Taylor

Second Edition
ISBN: 978-0-9981752-0-1

Cover and Book Design by James Woosley, FreeAgentPress.com

To Isla Rose

Table of Contents

Foreword

I REMEMBER IT LIKE IT was yesterday although it's been almost twenty years! Nancy was working for First Place 4 Health at the time. She and I were standing in the hall of our offices and she shared with me that she intended to memorize fifty-two verses that year. All during the year I asked her to say her verses for me and sure enough, at the end of that year, Nancy said all fifty-two verses with the references. To say that I was surprised would be an understatement. Not because she was able to do it but that she had kept her commitment for an entire year.

Because of Nancy's commitment, my assistant, Pat Lewis and I committed to memorize all the First Place 4 Health memory verses. We memorized the 200 memory verses in two years just by memorizing one verse a week as we walked side by side on the treadmills at our church. My life has been forever changed by the decision to memorize those 200 verses and because they are tucked so deep down in my heart, the Lord brings them to my remembrance when I speak, write and mentor women in the faith. Scripture memory is a big part of the First Place 4 Health program but many of our members memorize one verse a week but don't continue to practice saying it. If we continually practice the verses we have memorized and use them on a regular basis they become a part of the fabric of who we are.

I am eternally grateful for Nancy's faithfulness to continue memorizing Scripture all these years. Nancy has given me many verses, but two of my favorites are those she gave me after our daughter, Shari, was killed by a drunk driver, on Thanksgiving night, 2001. Romans 15:13 gave me hope and filled me with joy and peace because our God is the God of hope and Psalm 27:13 assured me that I would see the goodness of the Lord in the land of the living.

"MAY THE GOD OF HOPE FILL YOU WITH ALL JOY AND PEACE AS YOU TRUST IN HIM, SO THAT YOU MAY OVERFLOW WITH HOPE BY THE POWER OF THE HOLY SPIRIT."

Romans 15:13

"I AM STILL CONFIDENT OF THIS: I WILL SEE THE GOODNESS OF THE LORD IN THE LAND OF THE LIVING."

Psalm 27:13

I have watched as day after day, month after month and year after year Nancy faithfully shows up at our church's fitness center and practiced her verses while on the treadmill each morning. Nancy has inspired me, and so many others, to keep at it and never stop memorizing God's Word.

My prayer is that this book mobilizes Christians everywhere to begin memorizing one verse a week because the day could come when the only Scripture we have is what we have hidden in our heart.

Thank you, Nancy, for modeling for us all how we can learn to do what you do.

Carole Lewis
Director Emeritus, First Place 4 Health
Author of *Give God A Year*

Introduction

AT H.O.M.E. IN MY HEART

*G*OD'S WORD IS AT long last at home in my heart. I can now say that **hiding** His Word in my heart has enabled me to take **ownership** of it, provided me many opportunities to **minister** to those who are weary or brokenhearted, and most importantly, it has allowed me to **experience** a deeper, more intimate relationship with Christ.

After accepting Christ as my Savior as a child, I remained immature in my faith until I discovered the habit that would transform my life. I accepted Christ out of a desire to be safe and secure. I needed the security and peace that God offered and that I lacked as a child of an alcoholic father.

My dad was a wonderful, fun-loving man when sober, but he drank often and was verbally abusive when he was drunk. The years of storing up these defeating words in my mind wreaked havoc on me emotionally, mentally, and spiritually.

In my last year of college I discovered a whole new world of active Christians that were living out their faith and enjoying it! I had never experienced that before and I saw something in this group of people that I wanted desperately in my life. They prayed, read their Bibles, and talked about God working in their lives. As I became friends with them, I discovered what it meant to grow as a Christian. I was introduced to new disciplines such as daily devotions, Bible study, prayer journaling, and scripture memorization. The disciplines were just what I needed, or so it seemed, to gain that safety and security that had eluded me as a child and so the "roller coaster" ride of trying to live out my faith in Christ began.

I would keep up with these routines for a while, and then a crisis or an event would come along in my life that would interrupt my discipline. I was in the trap of "all or nothing" thinking. I believed a lie that said, "Nancy, if you can't perform perfectly, then just give up!"

God gently guided me out of this trap by showing me how to grip tightly to the Word of God, and in turn He totally transformed my life providing me with the safety and security I was seeking. Through **hiding** God's Word in my heart I took **ownership** of the truth that became my sword to cut away the lies I had believed. This truth has produced a wealth of wisdom that is available as I **minister** to those in need and as I personally **experience** a deeper, more intimate relationship with Jesus, the Word who became flesh! The Word is now permanently at **H.O.M.E.** in my heart.

When people saw how God's Word had changed my life, they would often ask me to conduct workshops or teach a class on how to develop the transforming habit of scripture memorization. Each time I taught, my passion grew for helping others to experience God's transforming Word. After each class at least one person would ask me if I had a book explaining in more detail my process of memorizing the Word.

After years of people asking me this question I decided it was time to write it. This book is a result of my passion for hiding God's Word in my heart and a desire for sharing this passion with others.

How to Get the Most Out of This Book

I AM HUMBLED AND GRATEFUL that you have my book in your hands! Now my prayer is that it will inspire, challenge and equip you to tighten your grip on God's Word.

I want to encourage you to read it, highlight anything that speaks to you directly, and above all else begin your own journey of taking God's Word to heart.

You can work through this book alone, with one whom you are mentoring, or with a small group of people who also desire to experience transformation through memorizing scripture.

Take a week to read through each chapter and work through the *Taking it to Heart* sections as a way to apply what you have read. Share what you are learning with your family, friends and co-workers.

I would also love to hear how God's memorized Word has transformed your life. Join the Taking the Word to Heart Facebook group to share your scripture memory journey and to receive encouragement and accountability.

Keep Feasting on His Word!

Nancy Taylor
Jeremiah 15:16

 facebook.com/groups/TakingTheWordtoHeart

 twitter.com/provetheword

 www.provetheword.org

 instagram.com/provetheword

"TAKE THE ... SWORD OF THE SPIRIT, WHICH IS THE WORD OF GOD."

Ephesians 6:17

Part 1

GETTING TO KNOW GOD
AND HIS WORD

MY JOURNEY FROM DEFEAT to delight began when the Lord showed me that the only weapon I needed in my quest to live a victorious life was the *memorized* Word of God. As I reached out to tighten my grip on God's Word, I was finally able to get off the roller coaster of my "all or nothing thinking."

I was in a Bible study that dealt with tearing down strong-holds and discovered that my biggest stronghold was my thought life. My mind continually cycled back into negative and destructive thoughts that had kept me from experiencing the life God had planned for me.

Once aware of my stronghold, I made an unwavering commitment to store up the weapon of the Word so that I would have an ample supply of ammunition against the enemy and his destructive lies that had taken captive my thought life! I made a commitment to memorize one verse a week for fifty-two weeks, with the goal of quoting all fifty-two verses at the conclusion of that time period. Never could I have conceived what God had in store for me through this simple commitment to memorize scripture and take His Word to heart. My knowledge of God increased, and along with this knowledge, my heart was filled with the love for God that Deuteronomy 6:5 speaks of:

> *"Love the Lord your God with all your heart and with all your soul and with all your strength."*

What began as a commitment to do something for myself became all about what God wanted to do in me through the Word that I had memorized and treasured in my heart.

He not only transformed my way of thinking, but also taught me how to delight in His truth when faced with daily inconveniences as well as life's overwhelming circumstances. In the English dictionary you will find that delight means "to give great joy or pleasure to; to be highly pleased, rejoice." However, in Hebrew, the language of the Old Testament, there are several words that are translated as delight which have richer meaning.

One such word, *chapets*, is found in Psalm 1:2, "His delight is in the law of the Lord," and means "a valuable thing." One who places great value in God's Word experiences delight. The word *chapets* is later found in scripture in Psalm 40:8 (NASB), "I delight to do Your will, O my God; Your law is within my heart," and refers to one being "inclined to do something" or "bending to it."

In Psalm 37:4, the familiar exhortation to "delight yourself in the Lord" is translated from the Hebrew word *anag*, meaning "to be soft or pliable." When I tied these meanings and verses together, I came to the conclusion that when one delights themselves in the Lord and in His Word, they are valuing God's Word in such a way that they are inclined to have a pliable heart and mind to live out the truths of God's Word.

I have learned to delight in His Word and have been amazed at how His truths flow from my mouth even when I find myself in a stressful or overwhelming circumstance. On the contrary, when I have delighted in the hard circumstances of my life by having a pity party, then what flows from my mouth are angry, bitter or harsh words.

We become like what we delight in, and if we delight in whining and complaining, then we become a whiner or a complainer when we find ourselves in a difficult situation. Luke 6:45 (NASB), "... for his mouth speaks from that which fills his heart," became real to me and I became delighted to speak truth into every difficulty. Jesus instructs us to listen to what He says and not to our natural inclinations in Matthew 5:44 (NASB), "But I say to you, love your enemies and pray for those who persecute you."

That is not natural, but spiritual. It means having a pliable heart and an opened mind to hear God's Word above your own thoughts. My mind was more attuned, my heart more moldable, and my ears more sensitive to the voice of Christ rather than my own self-focused thoughts when I consistently kept the commitment to weekly delight in God's Word.

Destructive, discouraging, and depressing thoughts do not come along as often, and when they try to invade my life, I have learned to use the weapon of God's Word to fight against those thoughts.

> ## "THE WEAPONS WE FIGHT WITH ARE NOT THE WEAPONS OF THE WORLD. ON THE CONTRARY, THEY HAVE DIVINE POWER TO DEMOLISH STRONGHOLDS."
>
> *2 Corinthians 10:5*

When I feel unattractive and worthless I am able to recall the truth of Psalm 139:14 that says, "I praise you because I am fearfully and wonderfully made. Your works are wonderful, I know that full well."

If I get discouraged after several attempts to finish a project, I can declare the truth of Micah 7:8, "Do not rejoice over me, O my enemy! Though I fall, I will rise. Though I dwell in darkness, the Lord is a light for me." (NASB)

When I experience loss or depressing thoughts overwhelm me, I have learned to go quickly to the comforting words of Psalm 62:8, "Trust in him at all times, O people; pour out your hearts to him, for God is our refuge."

God has revealed to me that if I am depressed, it is because I am more impressed with my own overwhelming circumstances than with Him and His powerful Word. God continues to show me that I must not believe or rationalize the lies of the enemy, but realize His truth when confronted with temptations, character flaws, and challenging events in my life. It is as if God is holding out His Word and saying to me, "Get a grip on my truth!"

When I am obedient to dwell on the truth hidden in my heart, I find that His truth, in turn, gets a grip on my thoughts, emotions, and even my behavior.

"I HAVE HIDDEN YOUR WORD
IN MY HEART THAT I
MIGHT NOT SIN AGAINST YOU."

Psalm 119:11

Chapter One

MEMORIZE:
MANNED WITH A PURPOSE
AND A PLAN

UST AS IT TAKES five fingers to have a good grip on what is being held in one's hand, it also takes five essential parts to provide a solid grip on the truth of God's Word. As I began my fifty-two week journey to memorize scripture, I discovered that memorization was just the beginning step and would only provide minimal strength to my grip. It was as if I was trying to hold a large suitcase using only my pinky! However, the pinky finger is an essential part of a solid grip; as is the act of memorizing the verses, which is merely the first step to completing the process of gripping God's Word.

Manned with a Purpose

Knowledge of God

Through memorizing scripture, we will gain a greater knowledge of who this God is that we are instructed to love with all our heart, soul, and strength (Deuteronomy 6:5). Not only will God's Word help us become better acquainted with God as our mighty God but also as our Counselor, who instructs us.

> *"For to us a child is born, to us a son is given and the government will be on his shoulders. And he will be called Wonderful Counselor, Mighty God, Everlasting Father, Prince of Peace." (Isaiah 9:6)*

> *"I will praise the LORD, who counsels me; even at night my heart instructs me." (Psalm 16:7)*

His Word gives us the knowledge that God will provide for our spiritual and physical needs.

> *"His divine power has given us everything we need for life and godliness through our knowledge of him who called us by his own glory and goodness." (2 Peter 1:3)*

The Word was written to teach us about the God who gives hope.

> *"For everything that was written in the past was written to teach us, so that through endurance and the encouragement of the Scriptures we might have hope." (Romans 15:4)*

God's Word was given to us by Him so that we can become like Him through its teaching, rebuking, correcting, and training in righteousness.

"All Scripture is God-breathed and is useful for teaching, rebuking, correcting and training in righteousness, so that the man of God may be thoroughly equipped for every good work." (2 Timothy 3:16)

In fact, God's Word is our life!

"When Moses finished reciting all these words to Israel, he said to them, 'Take to heart all the words I have solemnly declared to you this day, so that you may command your children to obey carefully all the words of this law. They are not just idle words for you---they are your life. By them you will live long in the land you are crossing the Jordan to possess.'" (Deuteronomy 32:45-47)

What better place to go than to God's Word to discover who this God is we are instructed to love! Knowledge of God is not only one of the purposes for memorizing scripture, but it is a life-changing benefit as well.

Memorizing scripture can become a legalistic action if done with the wrong motive. Chuck Swindoll has defined legalism as "conformity to a standard for the purpose of exalting self. The purpose of our discipline should be to order our lives in such a way that we are available to be used by God."[1]

In fact, Jesus warns us to "beware of practicing our righteousness before men to be noticed by them." (Matthew 6:1, NASB) Treasuring the Word in our hearts should be done with godly intention and purpose.

Other purposes for taking God's Word to heart include overcoming temptation, renewing and preparing the mind, receiving direction and guidance, developing godly character, and establishing an effective prayer life.

Overcoming Temptation

The New American Standard Bible translation states, in Psalm 119:11, that we are to "treasure" God's Word in our hearts, so that we will not sin against God. The New International Version states that the Word is "hidden" in our hearts. I have a problem with using the word hidden, as I have hidden many a Christmas present in July but have totally forgotten about it until sometime in January. Whereas, the word treasure reminds me of the strand of pearls given to me by my husband in honor of our fifteenth wedding anniversary.

Because I treasure those pearls, I keep them in a special velvet pouch tucked inside a wooden box for safekeeping. I keep them there so that I will know exactly where they are when I want to wear them. So it is with the Word of God.

When I am tempted to sin, the treasured Word of God is safely tucked in my heart, so that I will know where it is when I need it! I can still be overcome by temptation unless I cry out to God, seeking and asking Him to activate His Word in my life. When we cry out to Him, He will accomplish what concerns us.

> "I will cry to God Most High, to God who accomplishes all things for me." (Psalm 57:2, NASB)

God is so powerful and sovereign that He could just put in our minds and mouths a scripture that we had never memorized in our attempt to resist the enemy. However, I have never had that happen! It was only after I began to memorize scripture and ask God to use it in my life, that He would bring it to my mind and empower me to submit to His truth and resist the enemy.

Once I was exiting the freeway in pursuit of a forbidden dessert at one of my favorite restaurants, the treasured Word came roaring into my thoughts before I could act on the temptation. The truth of 1 Corinthians 10:13 pounded in my head:

> *"No temptation has seized you except what is common to man. And God is faithful; he will not let you be tempted beyond what you can bear. But when you are tempted, he will also provide a way out so that you can stand up under it."*

I cried out at that moment, "Lord, show me the way out!" As I drove onto the exit ramp, I stayed in the left-hand lane, taking a left turn that led straight to the safety of my home! The treasured Word was in my heart, just where I had put it for such a time as this.

Renewing and Preparing the Mind

Peter exhorts believers:

> *"Therefore, prepare your minds for action, be self controlled, set your hope fully on the grace to be given you when Jesus Christ is revealed." (1 Peter 1:13)*

A couple of years ago, I ran my first and only half-marathon. I didn't show up on the day of the race without first preparing for six months. My goal was to finish the race and in a somewhat respectable time frame. As I began my preparation, my intention was to walk the entire 13.1 miles, but as I followed my daily plan, I became stronger and began jogging a mile here and there along the way. In the month before the race, it became evident to me that I could possibly run at least half of the 13.1 miles.

On the day of the race, I paired up with a young friend of mine who had trained to run the full length of the race. As we made our way to the starting line, she asked if I wanted to run with her and I reluctantly agreed, knowing that I probably wouldn't be able to keep up with her pace for more than a couple of miles.

We were encouraged, as we ran along the course, by people holding banners and shouting, "You can do it!" Before I knew it I had run nine of the 13.1 miles and finished the race in a much better time than I had anticipated! Preparing my body and mind for the race gave me the strength to not only compete, but to finish well.

> *"Therefore, since we are surrounded by such a great cloud of witnesses, let us throw off everything that hinders and the sin that so easily entangles and let us run with perseverance the race marked out for us." (Hebrews 12:1)*

Prior to my scripture memory journey, my mind was filled with such self-destructive thoughts as, "I will never be good enough," or "God would never forgive me for that," and even "I am too old to change now!" I began not only to believe those lies, but my behavior began to mimic my thought life. Instead of walking in confidence I was walking in shame and defeat.

A popular computer phrase, *Garbage in, garbage out*, also illustrates how the human brain functions when continually fed with lies. Conversely, Scripture teaches, *Truth in, truth out.* Romans 12:2 commands:

> *"Do not conform any longer to the pattern of this world, but be transformed by the renewing of your mind. Then you will be able to test and approve what God's will is— his good, pleasing, and perfect will."*

In order to renew my mind I had to replace the lies with God's truth. The battle is won or lost in the mind!

Scripture clearly lays out our battle plans:

> *"We demolish arguments and every pretension that sets itself up against the knowledge of God, and we take captive every thought to make it obedient to Christ." (2 Corinthians 10:5)*

My dog loves to take me for a walk! He drags *me* along on *his* leash for as long as he can get away with it. Eventually I tug on the leash and command him to heel or sit! In the same way, we must renew our undisciplined thinking by taking command of the leash of every thought and intentionally aligning it with the truth of God's Word.

We must be prepared with the proper leash of God's truth if we want to captivate our thoughts with scripture. The only way we will be able to renew our minds is to have the Word stored up in our hearts. The Word that is at home in our hearts prepares us for the life-path that God gives each of us.

"I HAVE CHOSEN THE WAY OF TRUTH;
I HAVE SET MY HEART ON YOUR LAWS.
I HOLD FAST TO YOUR STATUTES,
O LORD; DO NOT LET ME BE PUT TO
SHAME. I RUN IN THE PATH OF YOUR
COMMANDS, FOR YOU HAVE SET MY
HEART FREE."

Psalm 119:30-32

When we use the Spirit-given self-controlled leash needed to prepare each day, our eyes become fully fixed on the knowledge of Christ. And having that knowledge will give us great encouragement because we begin to understand the love He has for us and the amazing grace that He willingly gives us. It is His grace that allows us to finish the race set before us. However, in order to run your race well, your mind must be renewed and prepared.

Gaining Direction and Guidance

Seeking to gain discipline in my eating habits, I memorized Titus 2:11–12, "For the grace of God that brings salvation has appeared to all men. It teaches us to say 'No' to ungodliness and worldly passions and to live self-controlled, upright and godly lives in this present age." The NASB put it another way: "to live sensibly, righteously and godly."

I was determined to say no to overeating and was able to accomplish this goal by renewing my mind with His Word, but the Lord had yet another use for His truth. After losing a good amount of weight, I rediscovered the joy of shopping. As I was preparing for some upcoming speaking and teaching opportunities, I realized that I needed some new clothes to fit my new body shape. As I shopped for the events, it seemed that everything I took into the dressing room fit perfectly and looked great on me. To borrow a sport phrase, "I was in the zone!"

Since everything was on sale, I rationalized that I could buy it all and so I did! It wasn't until I was standing in my closet looking at all I had bought that the Holy Spirit brought to mind Titus' words. I was convicted and then sought God's guidance, which I admit I was a little late in seeking, by asking Him if my purchase was sensible, righteous, and godly. Using God's Word as my counsel, I determined I should take half of my purchases back that day. As I did, a huge burden of guilt was lifted off of my shoulders and I knew God had directed my steps very clearly through His Word that I had treasured in my heart.

God created you with purpose and for a purpose. His purpose is to love us and be loved by us. Recently I heard someone say that we are God's dream come true! Psalm 139:16 tells us that our Creator wrote down all the days we were to live before we ever breathed our first breath! He knit us together while still in our mother's womb. He knows the days we live and will live and what those days will bring.

Therefore, since we are learning that He has ordained our days and given us everything we need for our life through our knowledge of Him (2 Peter 1:3), and knowing that knowledge comes straight from His Word, we can be assured that His Word will give us the guidance and direction we need to live this life well. A verse I pray back to God often is Psalm 143:8:

> *"Let the morning bring me word of your unfailing love,*
> *for I have put my trust in you. Show me the way I should*
> *go, for to you I lift up my soul."*

He counsels us with His love and gives us direction as we trust Him and grip tightly His instructive, loving, and living Word.

Developing Godly Character

I often will read one Psalm and one Proverb a day for my daily devotional. While the Proverb brings me conviction, the Psalm brings me compassion. Putting the two together reminds me of God's amazing power to convict through the Holy Spirit, and in the same moment, bring His compassion to soften the blow.

One morning I read Proverbs 14:23:

> *"In all labor there is profit, but mere talk leads only to poverty."*

Those divine words pierced my heart and showed me that I was not living a life of integrity at work. I was teaching people to commit to discipline their lives mentally, emotionally, physically, and spiritually, but I was failing to do the very things I was teaching.

I was just talking the talk and not walking the walk. That morning, I shared this scripture with those I worked with and confessed my character poverty. It was just a short time later that I began to memorize God's Word with a passion and with the motivation of this very verse, I realized I no longer wanted to be just a talker but also a doer of God's Word. The Lord continues to use this hidden treasure in my life to remind me to work and live with integrity.

Peter acknowledges that God gives us "his very great and precious promises . . . so that through them we may participate in the divine nature and escape the corruption in the world caused by evil desires" (2 Peter 1:4).

In other words, God's Word equips us for a new way of living. God recreates us once we receive the gift of salvation and we are made new in His eyes. We take on the righteousness of God first by simply responding to His call of redemption. Then once we have responded, we become new creatures, baby believers in Christ Jesus.

> *"Therefore, if anyone is in Christ, he is a new creation; the old has gone, the new has come!" (2 Corinthians 5:17)*

We must crave His Word—pure milk—so that we can grow up and mature.

> *"Like newborn babies, crave pure spiritual milk, so that by it you may grow up in your salvation." (1 Peter 2:2)*

In his letter to the church in Colosse, Paul informs the Colossians that Epaphras wrestled in prayer for them so that they would stand firm in all the will of God, mature and fully assured. (Colossians 4:12) In my own life, maturity has come only when I have been obedient to walk out the truths of God's Word. It is not easy, but it will produce a harvest of right living to those who have been trained by it. We discipline ourselves, not for discipline's sake, but for the joy set before us—the harvest.

> *"Let us fix our eyes on Jesus, the author and perfecter of our faith, who for the joy set before him endured the cross, scorning its shame, and sat down at the right hand of the throne of God." (Hebrews 12:2)*

> *"No discipline seems pleasant at the time, but painful. Later on, however, it produces a harvest of righteousness and peace for those who have been trained by it." (Hebrews 12: 11)*

Cultivating an Effective Prayer Life

While memorizing John 15:7 (NASB), I had an "aha" moment in which I discovered another purpose for hiding God's Word in my heart.

As I meditated on the words "If you abide in Me, and My Words abide in you, ask whatever you wish and it will be done for you," it became clear to me that praying the truths and promises of God's Word would result in praying God's will for my life. I began to attach people and their prayer needs to my memory verses. This helped me to keep my prayers focused and in line with God's will.

At fifteen years old, my son was drawing more and more into himself and was very depressed. I felt that the only way he would come out of his darkness was to grasp just how much God loved him. I cried out to the Lord and He showed me a scripture passage to pray for him. I quickly memorized the verses by praying them daily and also asking all the prayer warriors I knew to pray the same scriptures for him as well. That God would grant my son, "according to His glorious riches, to be strengthened with power through His Spirit in the inner man … being rooted and grounded in love … able to comprehend … the breadth, and length, and height, and depth of God's love." (Ephesians 3:16–19, NASB)

Through praying the powerful, life-changing truth of God's Word, my faith was strengthened, and my prayer life was refocused. Within a few weeks, my son's life took a dramatic turn. He came out of his depressed state and the joy of the Lord became so evident that before the year was out, he was leading worship at his high school's weekly chapel services.

Many years later I also prayed God's powerful Word on behalf of my daughter, Sarah. As she was approaching her graduation from law school I began to pray Psalm 90:17 over her life:

> *"May the favor of the Lord our God rest upon us;*
> *establish the works of our hands for us—Yes, establish the*
> *work of our hands."*

I was asking God's favor to rest on my daughter as she studied for the bar exam and to direct her to where she would be practicing law. During the three months she spent preparing,

I spent praying. Finally, the first morning of the three-day test arrived! However, she had fallen extremely ill over night and instead of receiving an excited phone call that the time had come, I received an emotional call for encouragement and help. I told her I had prayed for her Psalm 90:17 and that God would see her through.

She went to the exam that day and by God's grace and favor completed day one. He also sent her friends that brought her soup and medicine that evening. Each day she grew stronger, but felt that there was no way she would pass after that first day of sickness. It was another three months before she got the results of the test. We all gathered around the computer via Skype to be with Sarah, as she looked online for her exam results. I will never forget her words, "Thank you Jesus!" She had passed the bar exam and from that day on God has established her work as a criminal defense attorney.

"On the day I called, You answered me; You made me bold with strength in my soul." (Psalm 138:3, NASB)

REFLECTION

Take a moment to reflect on the purposes for taking God's Word to heart and consider each one:

1. Do you need more understanding of God's character?

2. Are you struggling with overcoming a specific sin in your life?

3. Do you need guidance and direction in making an important decision?

4. Do you need to develop integrity, patience or humility?

5. Do you want to increase the effectiveness of your prayer life?

6. Which purpose stands out to you the most? Why?

_____

_____

_____

_____

_____

_____

_____

_____

Manned with a Plan

Just having the "want to" of scripture memory will not accomplish the goal of hiding God's Word in your heart for a lifetime. As someone once said, "If you shoot for nothing, that is exactly what you get!" If you want to memorize scripture, then establish a plan and work it out until it works for you. Think of it like shopping for a pair of shoes—sometimes it takes trying on a few different plans before you find one that fits your learning style or lifestyle.

I will share a plan with you that worked for me. Try it on and then keep what works for you and adapt the rest to fit your learning lifestyle. Also, when a pair of shoes wears out and no longer fits comfortably, you either take them to the repair shop to have them refurbished, or you throw them out and buy a new pair.

Therefore, if on your journey of memorizing scripture you find yourself in a rut, then change it up, refurbish your plan, or take on a totally new one. The idea is to stay on the journey and not allow the plan to hinder you from progress. Work it out.

What Verses Should You Memorize?

One time in my Sunday morning Bible study the teacher mentioned Micah 7:8, as a side note to the main lesson. I had been in a battle with a specific sin issue in my life and had experienced defeat when this verse came rushing into my ears and went straight to my heart. "Do not gloat over me, my enemy! Though I have fallen, I will rise. Though I sit in darkness, the LORD will be my light."

I began memorizing the verse that very day and have been quoting it ever since, especially when faced with discouragement in the midst of momentary defeat. I suggest that you choose a scripture verse to memorize that has special meaning and purpose for your life.

For example, if you are struggling with a specific sin in your life and desire to have victory over that sin, then 1 Corinthians 10:13 would be a great place to start. When I am struggling with that old sin of overeating, this particular verse reminds me that there is a way out of the tempting situation. It says "No temptation has seized you except what is common to man. And God is faithful; He will not let you be tempted beyond what you can bear. But when you are tempted, He will also provide a way out so that you can stand up under it."

Memorizing scriptures that deal with certain topics such as God's character, relationships, marriage, God's will, peace, encouragement, and love may all be practical and relevant for your life but start by choosing scriptures that meet specific needs in your life or the lives of those you are praying for. This will help make it easier to memorize them and they will take root more quickly in your heart.

Keep a list of verses that you would like to memorize in your prayer journal, computer, or personal organizer/calendar. You will find that God pricks your heart and mind with scripture while in Bible study classes, listening to speakers or sermons, and while reading daily devotionals. When a verse speaks to you in a very personal and powerful way, then put it on the list of verses to memorize. Memorize verses that not only have special meaning and purpose, but also those that are immediately relevant to your life.

Ask God to show you in His Word one powerful truth that you can hide in your mind and heart that will encourage, inspire, or empower you in a specific struggle or concern you are dealing with now.

Search your Bible's concordance for verses related to your specific issue. Once you locate the verse that speaks directly to the heart of your need, write it here:

_____

_____

_____

_____

_____

To keep from setting yourself up for failure, it is best to stick with one to two verses a week. Once you become consistent and confident in your memorization, you may want to begin working on passages, chapters, or even entire books of scripture. I would never encourage someone to begin memorizing whole chapters before they got a handle on the verse-a-week system. Remember that it is not the quantity of verses you memorize, but the quality of life application you gain from each verse memorized.

What Translation Should I Use?

I began memorizing verses from the New American Standard Bible since it was the Bible I began using in college. It was easy to memorize due to its poetic language. However, I noticed that sharing these verses with un-churched friends and acquaintances seemed awkward because its use of Old English.

I eventually began to study and read mostly from the New International Version and found that it was more conversational—and thus more user-friendly—when sharing with nonbelievers. I would caution against memorizing large amounts of scripture from paraphrases, as they tend to be very wordy and are not always as biblically accurate as the translations. The key is to memorize from the version that you are most comfortable with and the one that you use most often.

What is My Plan?

Start With A Positive Attitude and A Spiral

Once you have a verse to memorize that is purposeful and practical in the version that you use regularly, then let the memorizing begin. Start with a positive attitude and a willingness to be intentional in your pursuit. Proverbs 14:23, one of the first scriptures I memorized, addresses the need to be intentional:

> *"All hard work brings a profit, but mere talk leads only to poverty."*

I reached a point where I was tired of just talking about my desire to memorize scripture and wanted to walk that desire out. When you string together several days of intentionally hiding God's word in your heart, it begins to develop into a habit.

I have found in my own life that I become what I habitually do. If I make a habit out of overeating, I become an overeater. If I make a habit of complaining, I become a complainer. Conversely, if I habitually thank God for each day's blessings, I become a grateful person and if I make a habit of memorizing scripture and walking it out in my life, I become a woman of the Word.

Once you intentionally make scripture memory a habit in your life, then you will become what Psalm 1 speaks of as "a tree planted by streams of water, which yields it fruit in season, whose leaf does not wither. Whatever he does prospers."

My fifty-two verses in fifty-two weeks plan began with spiral index cards. The spirals usually contain fifty 3x5" index cards. Since there are fifty-two weeks in a year, you will be able to carry this spiral with you for an entire year, enabling you to be constantly reminded of the verses you have memorized, as well as the one you are working on presently.

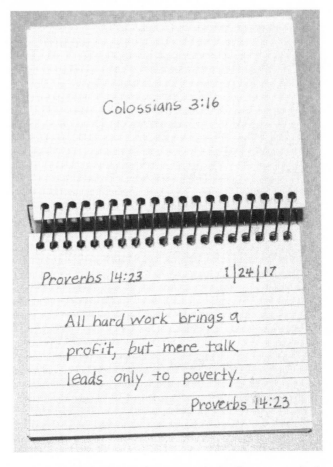

On each card, I wrote the scripture reference and the date on the top line. Knowing the reference is very important whenever the Lord gives you opportunity to share the verse with someone because this empowers them to go and look up the truth for themselves. Dating each card will give a timeline to when you memorized the verse and will help you associate the activity or season in your life with the verses you memorized. Then the scripture would be written on the following lines, with the reference written once again at the bottom of the card. On the back of the card, only the reference would be written. This will be helpful when reviewing the verses.

Determine Your Learning Style

I do my best thinking when I take my morning walks or when I am cleaning my house. Memorizing scripture while I am moving helps me to focus better on the words and their meaning. Recognizing how I learn best has helped me to continue on this scripture memory journey.

If you are an auditory learner, then singing the scripture memory verses, reading them aloud, or recording them will be very helpful in the memorization process.

If you are a visual learner, then writing the verses out and repeatedly reading through them will cement them into your mind visually.

If you are a tactile kinesthetic learner, or you learn by doing, then creating motions for the words or using sign language will enable you to more easily recall the verse.

Attach Daily Tasks to Scripture Memory

When my daughter was in high school she did not have a car, so I spent a good deal of time in the car with her as I carted her around to various activities. While in the car, I would have her quiz me on my verses. It was a great accountability tool and provided some teachable moments with my daughter, as well as some fun memories.

The bottom line is to make scripture memorization as much a part of your life as brushing your teeth or eating breakfast and as enjoyable as eating chocolate cake!

> "WHEN YOUR WORDS CAME, I ATE THEM; THEY WERE MY JOY AND MY HEART'S DELIGHT, FOR I BEAR YOUR NAME, O LORD GOD ALMIGHTY."
>
> *Jeremiah 15:16*

After determining your learning style, attach your scripture memorization to a daily task, whether it's driving your kids around, traveling to work, walking on the treadmill, or eating lunch. Use these daily tasks as opportunities to memorize and review your verses. Even meal times can be used as a time to share your verse with those at your table. Try closing email communications by typing in your weekly memory verse or make a point to say your memory verse every time you brush your teeth. These are just a few examples.

Read the Surrounding Verses

I had read and heard many times 1 Peter 5:7, "Cast all your anxiety on him because he cares for you."

This verse contains a wonderful truth that God cares for us and that we can trust Him to care for the things that bring us anxiety. However, I read the next verse and realized God was also telling me why to do this. 1 Peter 5:8 says, "Be self-controlled and alert. Your enemy the devil prowls around like a roaring lion, looking for someone to devour."

By simply looking at what follows casting my cares onto God, I see the urgency of the command. Casting our cares onto the Lord takes self-control and requires our alertness to our need to do so. His Word not only tells us what to do, but gives us the reasons we need to do it. When we carry our burdens around, we are weighed down and easily devoured by the enemy of depression, anger, and other such emotions that are contrary to what God would have us experience. God cares but the devil devours.

Before starting the actual memory work, read the entire passage that surrounds the verse you have chosen to memorize. This will give more insight and understanding into the verse and will guard against using the verse incorrectly or out of context. Reading the passage usually leads me to other verses that I write on my list of verses to be memorized, because they give me even more insight into God's Word and more ammunition to use against the enemy!

Paste the Reference to the Verse

For years I habitually said, "Somewhere in the Bible it says…" I knew the truth, but was unable to direct others to it and was unable to prove that what I was saying was in fact really in the Bible. It is crucial to paste the scriptural address to the verse as you memorize. When asked to provide your address to someone, you do not simply give the street, but also provide the street number. So it is with scripture. Knowing the reference gives credibility to the truth. Treat the reference of the verse like the first word of the verse.

For example, Romans 15:13 says, "May the God of hope fill you with all joy and peace as you trust in Him, so that you may overflow with hope by the power of the Holy Spirit."

When saying this verse over and over, always begin with "Romans 15:13" and do not pause before saying the first word of the verse. Say it just like you would your address. Saying the reference and the first few words as one phrase will help to attach the reference to those words, thus triggering you to remember the entire verse. Then repeat the reference at the end of the verse for added emphasis, like an exclamation point at the end of a sentence.

Once, as I was sharing a scripture reference followed by the verse with someone, they pointed out that my knowing the reference was so powerful and that it gave me credibility. She believed what I said because I backed it up with its location!

Associate the Reference

When memorizing Romans 15:13, I asked the Lord how could I remember those numbers. I noticed that the numbers fifteen and thirteen were the exact ages of my children. Teenagers are known for roaming around, so the reference was associated with roaming (Romans) teenagers, ages fifteen and thirteen. And since I was the mother of roaming teenagers, ages fifteen and thirteen, I needed the God of hope to fill me with all joy and peace! Thus this phrase, "Romans 15:13, May the God of hope," is cemented in my brain forever!

Once again, find a system that works best for you. Look for number patterns within the references, such as even or odd numbers, multiples, or sums. Sometimes it may come down to just repeating it over and over every day for a week before you can remember it. Writing only the reference on the reverse side of your scripture memory cards will also provide a convenient way to review your verses and paste the reference to them. You may want to make a list of the references with only the first three words of each verse. Write this in your prayer journal or on an index card to help you learn the order in which you memorized them. This will help to cement the reference to the first few words of each scripture. Remember to be intentional and ask God to help you find ways to associate the reference to the verse.

One Phrase at a Time

When memorizing Colossians 3:12, I used a "personal" technique for remembering the list of godly attributes God gives us in this verse. As I meditated on the words in the list, I noticed the first letters of each word were C, K, H, G, and P.

As I looked at C and K, I thought of my friend Kay, who always lavishes her friends with hugs. So C and K would stand for "See Kay." The H and G would stand for "hugs," and the P would remind me to say "please." So, C-K-H-G-P was attached to "See (C) Kay (K) for hugs (H, G), please (P)."

After spending the time to make this association, I have never forgotten that Colossians 3:12 says, "Therefore as God's chosen people, holy and dearly loved, clothe yourselves with compassion, kindness, humility, gentleness and patience."

Breaking a verse—especially one that is longer—into smaller phrases helps with the memorization process. As you read the phrases over and over, you may notice patterns, rhymes, or lists within the verse. Using different colored highlighters to highlight those key words and lists will also help cement the verse into your memory as you learn it and jog your memory as you review the verse.

Taking the time to search the memory verse for these patterns compares to building a house on a solid foundation. If you intentionally build a foundation of gluing the reference to the verse and breaking the verse into phrases as you search out patterns, rhyming words, and lists, the verse will stand strong in your mind, heart, and memory!

Perfectly

Learn each verse word-perfect. Have you ever noticed that when asked to recite the Pledge of Allegiance or sing a verse of "Amazing Grace," people will recite or sing the exact words? No one paraphrases the words, or says, "Well, it says something like…"

We all remember nursery rhymes and songs, such as "Mary Had a Little Lamb," learned in our childhood and can quote from memory the exact words. If I gathered a few of you in a room and asked you to sing that tune, most of you would sing it exactly the same. You learned the song perfectly, so you remember it perfectly!

Practice makes permanent. There is a degree of danger in this statement because we may well practice something incorrectly, and thus our practice becomes a bad habit. Practicing the exact words of scripture will insure that your practice will make perfect, enabling you to recall the words many years later.

We do not want to make scripture memory a legalistic task with no room for grace. However, we do want to hide the complete truth in our hearts, not just partial truth or a watered-down version. Take time to write out your verses correctly, not subtracting or adding any words. As you memorize the verse, and as you review it, take time to check your accuracy, so that you will know the whole truth and nothing but the truth!

Partner

When I got serious about memorizing scripture, I told all my friends about my goal to memorize a verse a week. I not only told them what I was doing, I also asked them to join my journey by holding me accountable. I asked friends and co-workers to make a point of asking me to quote the verse I was working on each week. And sometimes to my embarrassment, they followed through!

Accountability is an essential ingredient when developing any good or godly habit. Therefore, partner with someone as you seek to make scripture memorization a habit in your life.

"AS IRON SHARPENS IRON, SO ONE MAN SHARPENS ANOTHER."

Proverbs 27:17

It is important to ask at least one person who will encourage you in your journey and who will be faithful to ask you weekly for your memory verse.

One word of caution: It is best not to ask the one holding you accountable to also join you in memorizing scripture (assuming they are not already memorizing scripture), as sometimes that person will not hold you accountable when they are struggling with their own memorization. They could possibly not have the same level of commitment and thus may become a hindrance rather than a help to your journey. This will also avoid feelings of guilt or embarrassment. It is best to have a coach as an accountability partner and not necessarily a fellow teammate!

Persistent Review

As I write this book, I sit beside a basket full of scripture memory spirals. They are worn, torn, and stained. I have learned that if I keep them with me, the Word stays with me and I review them more often.

It has been said that it takes ninety to one hundred days of reviewing a verse before it truly becomes your own, or hidden in your heart. I find that using the index card spiral of fifty cards makes the review process much easier and more convenient. Sometimes, I will keep two spirals with me throughout the day—one contains the verses I am learning presently or during the current year, and the other contains verses from another year that I will review that day. The next day my current spiral continues to be my constant companion and I pick up another past year's spiral for a one-day review.

Review on a rotating basis, ensuring that you review verses older than one year at least once a week. Taking the verses with you wherever you go will be a constant reminder of your commitment to hide God's Word in your heart. Just like taking along a bottle of water on a long hike reminds you of your body's need for re-hydration, the memory verse spiral is a reminder that … "you do not live on bread alone, but on every Word of God" (Matthew 4:4).

Carry the verses with you so you will be ready to review while standing in line at the grocery store, while sitting in the waiting room at the doctor's office, or while relaxing during your afternoon break time. Intentionally use your free moments each day to soak your mind and heart in the truth by persistently reviewing your memory verses.

John Maxwell says, "Commitment is not an emotion; it is a character quality that enables us to reach our goals."[2] Do not allow your emotions to keep you from your commitment to hide God's Word in your heart.

Taking it to Heart

"No discipline seems pleasant at the time, but painful. Later on, however, it produces a harvest of righteousness and peace for those who have been trained by it."

Hebrews 12:11

Day One: Get Started!

1. Select a verse to memorize based on one of the purposes for scripture memorization: overcoming temptation, renewing and preparing the mind, receiving direction and guidance, developing godly character, or establishing an effective prayer life (see Appendix). Ask the Lord to reveal to you what area of your life needs the light of His truth.

_____

_____

_____

_____

2. Using an index card spiral, write the reference and date at the top of the first card. Write the verse and then write the reference at the bottom of the card. Then, read the entire chapter that the verse has been taken from to gain more insight.

3. Read the verse, breaking it into phrases, highlighting any key words, lists, or repeated words.

4. Connect the reference to the first few words. Locate patterns, phrases, or key words. Apply it to a current challenge or struggle. Pray the verse.

5. Read the verse slowly and with meaning. Repeat this several times until you can quote the verse without looking at it.

6. Carry the verse with you wherever you go and review while waiting in line, brushing your teeth, ironing your clothes, or walking on the treadmill.

Days Two–Six: Live Intentionally!

1. Repeat the process you completed on steps five and six of day one.

2. Pray and ask God for an accountability partner. Write down names of those who came to mind.

3. Seek out a partner who will faithfully hold you accountable by asking you to quote your verse for them at least once a week.

Day Seven: Review Day!

1. Try to write out the passage in your prayer journal or in the space provided below without looking at your index spiral. Check to see how you did. Make note of any special insights you discovered or ways you have practically applied the passage to your life.

_____

_____

_____

_____

_____

2. Review the verse throughout the day, striving for word-perfect memorization.

3. Intentionally share with one other person any application or insight you learned this week while memorizing your verse.

"Oh, how I love your law!
I meditate on it all day long.
Your commands make me wiser
than my enemies, for they are ever
with me. I have more insight than
all my teachers, for I meditate
on your statutes."

Psalm 119:97-99

Chapter Two

MEDITATE:
CHEW ON THE WORD AND
CONSIDER ITS MEANING

*M*EDITATION HAS HELPED ME to value *every word* of scripture. Taking time to focus on each word and asking the Lord questions about its purpose opens my eyes to a more personalized message of the Word. Psalm 18:28–29 says:

> "For You light my lamp; The LORD my God illumines my darkness. For by You I can run upon a troop; and by my God I can leap over a wall." (NASB)

While meditating on this verse, I read it over and over again, emphasizing a different word each time when the words "my darkness" pierced my heart. I suddenly realized afresh that darkness is not just out in the open, but it can be hidden within me. I have darkness, but God shines His light of truth on those dark thoughts, empowering me to overcome discouragement and concern. This helped me to gain further understanding—not only of the scripture but also of who God is and how He relates to me personally. I allowed the dark memories of my past to keep me from pressing forward in the future God had for me, but once this Word gripped my heart, freedom from the darkness came rushing in to give me renewed hope and vision.

If you have ever been in a play, choir program, or dance recital, you have experienced a dress rehearsal. A dress rehearsal is a final rehearsal, in full costume and with lights, music, and effects, before the production is given its first public performance. Meditating on scripture is a dress rehearsal for real life. When meditating on scripture, you are repeating the words and meaning of scripture daily in your mind. One Hebrew word for meditation means to muse, or rehearse in one's mind.[3]

The meditation process is especially helpful in memorizing scripture and applying it to real-life situations. As you meditate on scripture, you are also practicing how to live out the truth of what you are memorizing. It is "setting your mind on heavenly things" (Col. 3:1–2).

Memorizing scripture is just the pinky finger part of getting a grip on God's Word. The grip is strengthened when the ring finger is added. It is generally where we wear our wedding ring or class ring, which symbolizes commitment and accomplishment. Meditating on God's Word takes a commitment of time, but yields the accomplishment of a deeper knowledge of scripture. It is easy to become lazy in our walk with Christ and depend on others to constantly feed us spiritually. Meditation is the tool that will equip you to nourish yourself with the life-giving bread of God's Word.

The Meditation Process

Waylon Moore introduced me to his five-step meditation process in his book, *Living God's Word.*[4] By applying these steps I gained greater insight into the scriptures I was memorizing and my grip on the Word was tightened.

First Step: Perimeter of the Verse

I was memorizing John 16:33, "I have told you these things so that in me you may have peace. In this world you will have trouble. But take heart! I have overcome the world," and began to question what "these things" were Jesus spoke of that would bring peace.

Taking the time to read the prior verses, I discovered that He told the disciples He would send the Holy Spirit to guide them into all truth, reminding them of Jesus' words and of His love for them. Because of these things, we will experience the peace He speaks of in verse 33.

To begin the meditation process, relate the verse to be memorized with the verses surrounding it. In other words, we must be careful to not take a verse out of context, thus losing the intended meaning. Reading the full chapter surrounding the verse being memorized sheds light, gives insight, and helps broaden the scope of the verse. This is the same step used in memorizing, which was mentioned earlier. When reading the passage, be alert to observations and questions that may come to your mind. It is what my college English professor called "intentional reading."

Second Step: Paraphrase the Verse

A friend of mine always paraphrases her verses by putting her name in the verse or changing the word "men" to "women." As she paraphrases the verse, she makes it personal. A verse we memorized together was Proverbs 10:19, "When there are many words, transgression is unavoidable, but he who restrains his lips is wise." (NASB)

I was memorizing it to help with my weakness of talking when I should be quiet. My friend, however, attached it to her struggle with overeating and paraphrased it like this, "When there is much food around, overeating is unavoidable, but he who restrains his lips [literally!] is wise."

The Word spoke to both of us in different ways to meet specific issues in our lives. Writing the verse in your own words helps to cement the verse's meaning in your mind. Paraphrasing the verse makes it "yours" and gives you ownership of the Word. Thus, paraphrasing the verse will bring about more personal application.

Third Step: Pulverize the Verse

The meditation process has been compared to the process by which a cow chews on her cud. It is chewing on the Word over and over again. Pulverizing a verse allows you to spotlight each word contained in the verse. Repeatedly read the verse, each time emphasizing a different word, until you have highlighted each word. By the time you have read the verse that many times, you generally have it memorized!

As you read over the verse, one word may seem to leap off the page or "stand out" more than the others. Begin to ask yourself questions beginning with the words who, why, where, what, when, and how regarding the "standout" word. This is a great way to study scripture without any extra resources. It enables you to recall the verse more readily because you spent time with the verse and will have a personalized insight linked to the verse.

Fourth Step: Personalize the Verse

> *"Do not merely listen to the word, and so deceive yourselves. Do what it says." (James 1:22)*

This verse reminds me often to do what the Word says; not to just read or even memorize it, but to actually do it!

After you have a better understanding of the perimeter and have pulverized the verse, the Holy Spirit will begin to convict you of a sin or convince you of a truth that you need personally for an immediate challenge or circumstance. When this happens, apply the balm of the Word to that hurt, need, or challenge.

This is where transformation takes place—where we begin to deny ourselves, taking up our crosses and obediently following the Lord's Word and way.

Fifth Step: Pray the Verse

Praying the verse for yourself and others helps you to glue the truth of the memorized Word to specific needs in your life or others. Ask God to use the verse in your life each time you review it and to use it as a prayer reminder to pray for the needs of others as well.

The first year of my scripture memory journey I would associate each verse to a specific person. For example, Ephesians 6:11 became my husband's verse that I prayed for him daily as I reviewed it:

> *"Put on the full armor of God so that you can take your stand against the devil's schemes."*

I prayed daily for a young single woman whom I was mentoring Psalm 20:4, "May he give you the desire of your heart and make all your plans succeed." I still make it a habit to pray the verses I am reviewing as I walk on the treadmill daily. Praying your memory verses will cement their references and meanings in your mind, as well as empower and increase your prayer life.

You may want to repeat the meditation process for a few days or even the entire week in which you are memorizing the verse. I have not only used this process in my quiet times with the Lord, but also have used it as I waited in a doctor's office, as I drove my car, and as I exercised. You may copy the next page and place it with your scripture memory cards or in your prayer journal as a meditation guide.

THE MEDITATION PROCESS

Scripture reference: _____

Step One: Understand the perimeter of the verse

_____

_____

Step Two: Paraphrase the verse

_____

_____

Step Three: Pulverize the verse

Emphasize a different word in separate readings. Choose one word that is key to the message of the verse for you.

_____

Ask questions about the word and answer them if you can:

Who? _____

What? _____

When? _____

Where? _____

Why? _____

How? _____

Step Four: Personalize the verse

Apply the verse. Glue the promise to a problem.

_____

_____

Step Five: Pray the verse into your life

Ask God to make the verse a reality in your life today.

_____

_____

The Meditation Process form courtesy of Waylon B. Moore.

Taking it to Heart

"Since, then, you have been raised
with Christ, set your hearts on
things above, where Christ is
seated at the right hand of God.
Set your minds on things above,
not on earthly things."

Colossians 3:1–2

Day One: Pressing On!

1. Choose a new verse for this week and record it in your scripture memory index card spiral. Make the scripture memory plan work according to your personal learning style, changing it up to meet your needs. List ways you will personalize your plan.

_____

_____

_____

_____

_____

_____

_____

_____

2. Follow the meditation process throughout your week of memorizing the verse. You may make copies of the Meditation Process form located on page 45.

3. Review the previous week's verse each day as you learn a new one.

4. Take the index spiral or card with you wherever you go today and remember to attach your daily tasks to your scripture memory by reviewing the verse as you travel in your car, brush your teeth, do laundry, wait in line, before you eat each meal, and before going to sleep tonight.

Days Two–Six: Living Intentionally!

1. Repeat Day One exercises each day.

2. Look for opportunities to share the verse. Type it out each time you send an email (No copying and pasting!), share it on Facebook, Twitter, Instagram or try to work it into at least one conversation each day.

3. Give your mind an assignment as you go to bed each night. Try to quote as many memory verses as you can before falling asleep. In the morning, do not let your feet touch the floor until you attempt to quote your verse for the week.

Day Seven: Review Day!

1. Try to write out the passage in your prayer journal or in the space below without looking at your index spiral. Check to see how you did. Make note of any special insights you discovered or ways you have practically applied the passage to your life.

_____

_____

_____

_____

_____

_____

2. Contact your accountability partner and share your verse and how God used it in your life. Did it help in overcoming temptation? Did the truth of the verse convict you or sharpen your character in any way?

"THE SCRIPTURES WERE GIVEN
NOT TO INCREASE OUR KNOWLEDGE,
BUT TO CHANGE OUR LIVES."

D. L. Moody [5]

As we fall in love with the Lord, we desire to serve Him, which requires some of our own muscle. Application takes our strength—that is, realizing that our strength alone will not make us into a godly person, but it is our obedience to the power of God's Word.

> *"We demolish arguments and every pretension that sets itself up against the knowledge of God, and we take captive every thought to make it obedient to Christ." (2 Corinthians 10:5)*

We spend too much time rationalizing the lies of the enemy that say such things as, "You are not good enough" or "God could never forgive you." Instead we must start realizing God's truth that will set us free from the enemy's captivating lies.

> *"Then you will know the truth, and the truth will set you free." (John 8:32)*

Once I developed the discipline of memorizing and meditating on God's Word, I realized that in order to move forward in my journey of delighting in God, the Word had to rise up from my heart and overflow into the ruts of my life. The ruts are those selfish desires and actions that become ungodly habits that mark a person's life.

I began to ask God weekly to give me opportunities to apply His Word in my everyday circumstances. The truth of 2 Corinthians 3:18 became evident in my life, "and we who with unveiled faces all reflect the Lord's glory are being transformed into his likeness with ever increasing glory, which comes from the Lord, who is the Spirit."

His truth reveals the ungodly habits in our lives and as we turn toward that truth, the veil of sin that separates us from

Part 2

DEVELOPING A HEART OF OBEDIENCE

*I*N ORDER TO love the Lord with all our heart, soul, and might (Deuteronomy 6:5), we must get to know Him first through memorizing and meditating on His Word. Then Jesus takes our love a step further in John 14:21 when He says, "He who has my commandments and keeps them, he it is who loves me ..."

Memorizing and meditating is the heart and soul of Deuteronomy 6:5, while John 14:21 is the might! After rehearsing the truth through meditation, we take the stage of real life and live it!

God is removed. When the veil is removed, and we choose to walk in the truth of His Word, transformation takes place. We begin to reflect His glory! I have learned that obedience will only come when I admit my inability to change on my own. I cannot do anything without Him and His Word in me.

> *"I am the vine; you are the branches. If a man remains in me and I in him, he will bear much fruit; apart from me you can do nothing. If you remain in me and my words remain in you, ask whatever you wish and it will be given you." (John 15:5,7)*

I tried God's Word on and realized that I needed to make some alterations in my attitudes, thinking, and actions. He proved Himself to be the master tailor of my life.

> *"Rather, clothe yourselves with the Lord Jesus Christ and do not think about how to gratify the desires of the sinful nature." (Romans 13:14)*

When I put on the Lord Jesus Christ, He takes the scissors and needles of His Word and remakes me into a new creation, empowering me to overcome the challenges of life. Since the Word is Christ, we clothe ourselves with the truths and promises contained in the Word by first putting it into our minds and hearts and then walking it out.

"FOR ALL WHO ARE BEING LED
BY THE SPIRIT OF GOD,
THESE ARE SONS OF GOD."

Romans 8:14 - NASB

Chapter Three

MOBILIZE:
APPLYING THE WORD
TO YOUR LIFE

*S*O MANY TIMES in my life I have been caught in the trap of thinking that if things were going to change in my life then it was up to me, and me alone! I have tried to lose weight, to get along with difficult people, and even to get organized in my own strength. I would be successful for a little while, but eventually I would fall back into my old way of thinking and acting.

I needed a way to be constantly reminded of truth that would set me free. In my first year of memorizing scripture, I discovered that I had to live out a scripture in order for it to be cemented in my heart and mind.

The third finger of our grip is the tallest and strongest part of the grip. The third step in the process of taking His Word to heart is learning to apply the truths of scripture to our real-life circumstances and mobilize the Word into our life.

To mobilize means to organize resources to be ready for action. After memorizing and meditating on God's Word, your mind is prepared to actively obey its commands. Peter instructs us to prepare our minds for action.

> *"Therefore, prepare your minds for action; be self-controlled; set your hope fully on the grace to be given you when Jesus Christ is revealed." (1 Peter 1:13)*

James goes a step further when he exhorts us to not only listen to the Word—memorizing and meditating on it—but to actually do what it says.

> *"Do not merely listen to the word, and so deceive yourselves. Do what it says." (James 1:22)*

The purpose of obedience to God's Word is explained in 2 Peter 1:5-8:

> *"For this very reason make every effort to add to your faith goodness; and to goodness, knowledge; and to knowledge, self-control and to self-control, perseverance; and to perseverance, godliness, and to godliness, brotherly kindness, and to brotherly kindness, love. For if you possess these qualities in increasing measure, they will keep you from being ineffective and unproductive in your knowledge of our Lord Jesus Christ."*

To mobilize the Word into our lives we take what we have stored up in our minds and act on that knowledge. This action pleases God and transforms us into effective witnesses for Christ.

Proving the Word

The process of developing godliness begins with knowledge followed by applying self-control to what you know. When we do not discipline ourselves for godliness our lives begin to implode.

> *"Like a city whose walls are broken down is a man who lacks self-control." (Proverbs 25:28)*

Rebuilding the broken things in our lives takes God's grace and truth mixed with our application of self-control. I call this proving the Word. Proving the Word simply means taking the Word of God and practically applying it to your real-life circumstances by living the Word (James 1:22), praying the Word over a person or situation (John 15:7) and breaking the silence of lies through speaking the Word in response to whatever life brings your way.

Geometry was my favorite subject in high school. Most people groan whenever I disclose this fact. However, I think it was more about the teacher than the subject! One of the things I enjoyed was solving proofs. The teacher would write a statement on the chalkboard and then ask us to prove that statement true or false using the truths or theorems that we had been given.

In the same way, the Holy Spirit reminds us of what Jesus has said to us in His Word, and empowers us to live out those truths—proving them to be true.

> *"But the Counselor, the Holy Spirit, whom the Father will send in my name, will teach you all things and will remind you of everything I have said to you." (John 14:26)*

God gives us His Word and His Spirit, and then through specific circumstances He gives us the opportunity to prove it true through our obedience.

And with each opportunity comes a lesson straight from the heart of God meant just for us!

> *"I applied my heart to what I observed and learned a lesson from what I saw." (Proverbs 24:32)*

Proving the Word is another way to say, "Live by the Spirit." When I would hear a sermon on living by the Spirit and not by the flesh, I would get all pumped up, but then fall flat on my face by the next day. I didn't have a practical way of living by the Spirit. I need practicality.

> *"Those who live according to the sinful nature have their minds set on what that nature desires; but those who live in accordance with the Spirit have their minds set on what the Spirit desires." (Romans 8:5)*

Living by the Spirit starts with setting our minds on what the Spirit desires. This truth is practically illustrated in this story of a pilot as told by Neil Anderson in his devotional book, *Daily in Christ*:

THE HOLY SPIRIT'S GUIDANCE

A young pilot had just passed the point of no return when the weather changed for the worse. Visibility dropped to a matter of feet as fog descended to the earth. Putting total trust in the cockpit instruments was a new experience to him, for the ink was still wet on the certificate verifying that he was qualified for instrument flying.

The landing worried him the most. His destination was a crowded metropolitan airport he wasn't familiar with. In a few minutes he would be in radio contact with the tower. Until then, he was alone with his thoughts. His instructor had practically forced him to memorize the rule book. He didn't care for it at the time, but now he was thankful.

Finally he heard the voice of the air traffic controller. "I'm going to put you on a holding pattern," the controller radioed. Great! thought the pilot. However, he knew that his safe landing was in the hands of this person. He had to draw upon his previous instructions and training, and trust the voice of an air traffic controller he couldn't see. Aware that this was no time for pride, he informed the controller, "This is not a seasoned pro up here. I would appreciate any help you could give me."

"You've got it!" he heard back.

For the next 45 minutes, the controller gently guided the pilot through the blinding fog. As course and altitude corrections came periodically, the young pilot realized the controller was guiding him around obstacles and away from potential collisions. With the words of the rule book firmly placed in his mind, and with the gentle voice of the controller, he landed safely at last.

The Holy Spirit guides us through the maze of life much like that air traffic controller. The controller assumed that the young pilot understood the instructions of the flight manual. His guidance was based on that. Such is the case with the Holy Spirit: He can guide us if we have a knowledge of God's Word and His will established in our minds.[6]

To remember the scriptures I am memorizing, I realized that the verses would have to be proven to be true in my life. I would have to do what the Word says in order to protect myself from being simply a hearer and "quoter" of the Word. Using the meditation process as my starting point, I began to pray and ask God to use the verse in my everyday circumstances. I asked Him to open my eyes to opportunities to apply the memory verses to conversations, challenges, and even to my thought life. Looking closer into the verse, I would ask myself questions such as:

- Is there a sin to confess?

- Is there an action to take?

- Is there a command to obey?

- Is there a promise to claim?

I then began to record how God proved His Word through specific verses. I even kept a list on my computer entitled, "Scriptures God Has Proved in my Life."

Finally, I looked for opportunities to share these "proving experiences" with others. Proving the Word is an intentional act of the will. It is choosing to think, talk, and walk the way of truth (Ps. 119:30). Proving the Word isn't something that happens by accident, but with discipline and diligence.

Living the Word

I discovered a verse that revolutionized my attitude, and I hope it will do the same for you. Proverbs 15:15 says, "All the days of the afflicted are bad, but a cheerful heart has a continual feast." (NASB)

The week I was memorizing and meditating on this verse I was to fly to California to speak at a workshop. The morning my plane was to depart, I arrived at the airport two hours early due to all the extra security. I checked my bags and went through the security line with ease. It was going to be a great day!

Shortly after this thought went through my mind, I was greeted at the gate with the word "canceled" flashing at the check-in desk. The waiting area sat eerily vacant and my first instinct was to panic and enter into a really bad day. The Holy Spirit tapped me on the shoulder and the words of Proverbs 15:15 swept through my mind. I laughed out loud and then looked around to see if anyone had seen me!

God was up to something! He was calling on me to try His Word and see if it was true. So I took the challenge and set out to prove His Word. At that moment, I chose to have a cheerful heart and looked to see what feast might await me.

After standing in a long line for about thirty minutes, all the while rehearsing in my mind the truths of Proverbs 15:15, I discovered that all flights to Dallas had been canceled due to bad weather and my itinerary called for a stopover in Dallas before boarding a flight to Oakland. As I stepped up to the counter, I greeted the clerk with a smile, because I had chosen to be cheerful.

She said, "I am sorry, but you will have to change airlines, which means you will have to walk to baggage pick-up and then take a tram to another terminal to board your plane."

I replied cheerfully, "Not a problem, I didn't care for my original airline and I need the exercise!"

She continued with her bad news, "You will be on a non-stop flight, arriving in Oakland two hours early."

My dimples deepened as I grinned even bigger and said to myself, "Continual feast!" I got on the airplane and discovered that I had the entire row of seats all to myself. I was able to read, study, and rest for the entire three-hour flight. It was quite a feast! I had tried God's Word, chosen to obey its truth, and found it to be true. All those things probably would have happened with or without a cheerful attitude, but I would not have enjoyed God's blessings nearly as much if I had chosen not to ask God to prove His Word true in my life.

Praying the Word

I had an aha moment as I memorized John 15:7 (NASB):

> *"If you abide in Me and My words abide in you, ask whatever you wish, and it will be done for you."*

The phrase "My words abide in you" took on a whole new meaning as I mediated on the truth. If I am hiding God's Word in my heart, then when I ask the truth of His Word to be true in my life, God answers!

A powerful and sure way to prove the Word in your life is through prayer. As I pray and ask God to apply truth to my life, I also look for opportunities to pray the verse for others.

Psalm 107:20 became "Charlene's verse" once I received the heartbreaking news that she had been diagnosed with multiple sclerosis. The verse reminded me of the healing power of God's Word.

> *"He sent His word and healed them, and delivered them from their destructions." Psalm 107:20 (NASB)*

I began to pray, "Lord, send Your Word to Charlene, healing her and delivering her from destruction." I told Charlene that I was praying Psalm 107:20 for her each day. A couple of weeks later we passed one another in the hallway at church. She took hold of my arm and with great excitement said, "Nancy, you inspired me with your memorized scriptures and so now I want to memorize scripture. Whenever you see me, ask me to quote for you the verse I am memorizing."

I was so humbled to know that God used me as an instrument of inspiration in Charlene's life; but more amazing was how God was answering my prayer of sending His Word and healing Charlene. The answer did not look like I had anticipated—a miraculous healing. But God was sending His Word into Charlene's life as she hid it in her heart. Now I watch expectantly to see how His healing and deliverance will come!

Another example of the way God works is when I was asked to be a part of a small accountability group a few years ago with five other women. When I learned who would be leading the group I was a bit hesitant to join. I didn't know her well, but what I knew about her led me to believe she would be a rigid and strict leader. I was fearful that if I joined the group I would be miserable but through the encouragement of friends I put aside my pride and assumptions and joined the group.

Later the leader of the group attended one of my classes on scripture memory and as a result she and her husband began to memorize scripture together. She shared this with me and asked me if I wanted to walk with her a couple of times a week for the purpose of reviewing our scriptures and praying together.

As time went on I began to really enjoy my time with her. One week I was memorizing 1 Peter 1:22 and as I quoted it to her on one of our walks, my heart just about leaped out of my chest! It says, "Now that you have purified yourselves by obeying the truth so that you have sincere love for you brothers, love one another deeply from the heart."

The weeks that my friend and I had walked, prayed, and shared together how we were applying our memory verses, God had purified my heart of its rebellious assumptions and given me a sincere love for her. Now I love her deeply from my heart! The Lord had proved His Word true in my life once again.

Speaking the Word

As I was waiting for my turn to speak at an event, I listened to three women give their testimonies of how God had been working in their lives. As the first woman gave the details of her story, one of my memory verses came rushing into my mind. I had a divinely given urge to share the scripture with this woman. However, since I was in the audience with hundreds of people, I simply wrote it down so that I could share it with her afterwards. Then the same thing happened with the second woman, and then again with the third. The Lord gave me specific scriptures of hope and encouragement for each woman.

When the time came for me to walk to the podium to speak, I had to first tell everyone of this wonderful revelation. I stood at that moment and told each woman the verse the Lord had given to me especially for them and their circumstances. That evening after I spoke, all three women came to ask again where their verse was found and to thank me for sharing the truth with them. As I drove home, I praised the Lord for giving me the ability to hide His Word in my heart—not for my sake, but for those who crossed my path that night.

I could say with Isaiah, "The Sovereign Lord has given me an instructed tongue, to know the word that sustains the weary. He wakens me morning by morning, wakens my ear to listen like one being taught" (Isaiah 50:4).

Jesus instructed His disciples, "What I tell you in the dark, speak in the daylight; what is whispered in your ear, proclaim from the roofs." (Matthew 10:27) There is power in speaking the Words of God.

Micah knew that power when he said in Micah 7:7–8:

> *"But as for me, I will watch expectantly for the Lord. I will wait for the God of my salvation. My God will hear me. Do not rejoice over me, O my enemy. Though I fall I will rise; though I dwell in darkness, the Lord is a light for me." (NASB)*

Micah spoke the truth of who God is aloud to the circumstance. In fact, I memorized Micah's words to proclaim aloud the truth that God is light whenever I find myself in a dark situation.

The enemy wants to discourage us when we fail or relapse into sinful habits. Proclaiming aloud this verse gives me hope and power to move out of the darkness of my sin into the forgiving light of God's grace.

David also knew the power of crying out to God. He spoke not only his requests for deliverance, but also his proclamations of the truth of God's character.

> *"I will cry to God Most High, to God who accomplishes all things for me." (Psalm 57:2, NASB)*

Jesus told His disciples that although He would leave them physically, God was going to send a Counselor who would be with them always and would even remind them of everything He had told them when He was with them. (John 14:26)

When we hide the Word in our hearts, it takes root and remains within our storehouse of truth. Then, when faced with challenges or temptations, the Holy Spirit will tap on the shoulder of our heart and speak softly the truth we have hidden there. It is then our part to apply it as a healing balm to a wound or a word of wisdom to a friend.

"Let the word of Christ dwell in you richly as you teach and admonish one another with all wisdom and as you sing psalms, hymns and spiritual songs, with gratitude in your hearts to God." (Colossians 3:16)

This third step of gripping the Word of God is the strongest and perhaps the most character molding of the grip. Memorizing the Word gives us the knowledge of the Word, while meditation brings that knowledge to light in our own lives, giving us understanding. Then, understanding gives us fuel for mobilizing the Word into our lives through living it out, praying it, and speaking it. It moves us from being simply a member of the audience of Christianity to the stage of life where we actively participate in working out the truth of Christianity for His purpose and pleasure.

"For it is God who is at work in you, both to will and to work for His good pleasure." (Philippians 2:13, NASB)

It is what living a life of obedience is all about—experiencing His Word working in us!

"And we also thank God continually because, when you received the word of God, which you heard from us, you accepted it not as the word of men, but as it actually is, the word of God, which is at work in you who believe." (1 Thessalonians 2:13)

TAKING IT TO HEART

"DO NOT MERELY LISTEN TO THE WORD
AND SO DECEIVE YOURSELVES.
DO WHAT IT SAYS."

James 1:22

Day One: Pressing On!

1. Choose a new scripture for this week. Pray, asking God to prove this scripture in your life in a very practical way. Ask Him to reveal new insights into this verse.

_____

_____

_____

_____

_____

_____

_____

_____

_____

_____

_____

2. Use the meditation process to cement this verse in your mind. Make another copy of the Meditation Process to use as you meditate on your new verse.

3. Take the spiral with you wherever you go today and review the verse as you travel in your car, brush your teeth, do laundry, wait in line, before you eat each meal, and before going to sleep tonight. Look for opportunities to prove the verse true throughout your day.

Days Two–Seven: Living Intentionally!

1. Connect with your accountability partner and share your new verse.

2. Pray the verse for yourself and others.

3. Share the verse with someone each day as an encouragement, in an email, a telephone conversation, or a note.

4. Be alert to opportunities to prove the verse in your life.

5. Find motivation through short-term goals. For example, give the gift of the memorized Word to someone special. Quote your memory verses as a blessing for an individual or for a family member's birthday or special occasion.

"THOSE WHO KNOW YOUR NAME
WILL TRUST IN YOU, FOR YOU,
LORD, HAVE NEVER FORSAKEN
THOSE WHO SEEK YOU."

Psalm 9:10

Part 3

LIVING A LIFE OF TRUST

*E*ARLY ONE MORNING, my daughter and I were driving to the state high school baseball championship game. The further we drove, the darker the sky grew as the threat of severe weather surrounded us. Before we knew it, we were in the midst of a dangerous storm with heavy rain, wind, and lightning. Fear gripped both of us as we sought to find shelter from the storm. Piercing my heart and flooding my mind were the words of Psalm 91:1, "He who dwells in the shelter of the Most High, will rest in the shadow of the Almighty." (NASB) I began to shout those words over and over until the rest came to my heart as I was reminded of the Lord with whom I trusted my very life.

As we seek to know the Lord we are commanded to love, we find that our obedience brings about blessing. Through experiencing God in our seeking to know Him more intimately and obeying His Word, we discover firsthand the trustworthiness of God. The God who promises is faithful to fulfill those promises!

> *"God, who has called you into fellowship with his Son Jesus Christ our Lord, is faithful." (1 Corinthians 1:9)*

The more we memorize, meditate on, and mobilize God's Word into our lives, the more childlike our faith becomes. We trust Him, no matter what the circumstance. As we take in His Word consistently, we begin to take on the responsibilities and rewards of being His chosen ones.

> *"For no matter how many promises God has made, they are "Yes" in Christ. And so through him the "Amen" is spoken by us to the glory of God." (2 Corinthians 1:20)*

Our lives become marked by God's Word and work in our lives.

"BE IMITATORS OF GOD, THEREFORE,
AS DEARLY LOVED CHILDREN AND LIVE
A LIFE OF LOVE, JUST AS CHRIST LOVED
US AND GAVE HIMSELF UP FOR US
AS A FRAGRANT OFFERING AND
SACRIFICE TO GOD."

Ephesians 5:1,2

Chapter Four

MARKED:
BEING TRANSFORMED
BY THE WORD

THE WORD HAS marked my life. As Jeremiah was known by others as the man of the Lord of Hosts, I desire to be known by others, not as Nancy, the mother of Sarah and Will or the wife of William or even the Bible study teacher, but as the woman of the Lord of Hosts: A woman of the Word. Hiding God's Word in my heart has given me ownership of His Word. I remember so vividly when I came to the realization that God's Word had become my Word. I was sitting in a church service and as the pastor began to read the text for his sermon, it was as if he was reading my prayer journal. Those were my scriptures; scriptures that I had hidden in my heart and that had been proven true in my life!

Another moment that proved to me that God's Word had become my Word came to me as I was wearily making the long trek home in Houston traffic. My eyes were glazed over as I half-heartedly listened to the Christian radio station playing on my car stereo. Then the deejay began interviewing a man who was to be one of the worship leaders that evening at a citywide praise and worship service.

My ears perked up as I heard the worship leader say, "I have spent time developing my secret life." That got my attention and I wanted to know more.

The deejay asked, "Is it true that you have never completed a college degree, but have been a worship leader for nineteen years?" The worship leader answered, "I have never had to promote myself. The scripture tells us that what is done in secret will be revealed. So I have just worked on my secret life. I started by getting alone in my room as a teenager to sing and play the guitar to the Lord. Then I would sing to the Lord or take a walk and pray. This became a habit and my secret life was revealed as I publicly led others in worship."

By this time, I was looking for something to write on as I drove down the freeway. "Wow!" I thought, "That is how you live a marked life and this is what has happened to me!" I had set out to memorize God's Word to renew my mind and increase my ammunition against the enemy, but something greater occurred. The secret times I spent hiding scripture in my heart became evident to those who my life touched. The pointer finger is used to show direction or point out something that you want someone else to see. In the same way the fourth step, *marked*, reveals how God's Word transforms a person from the inside out.

Gripping God's Word through memorizing, meditating, and mobilizing it in your life will make a profound mark on your life. I have found that God's treasured Word has marked my life spiritually, relationally, and publicly.

When the Word has been implanted within your mind and heart, it acts as a gardener. The Word is sharp, so it is a hoe that breaks up the hard places of our hearts, making them more accessible to the seeds of faith God wants to sow in us. When the Word breaks up our hearts, we become more aware of the sin that is trying to take root.

I find I keep shorter accounts with God, in that my heart is more fertile, allowing conviction to come easier—and God's Word is Miracle-Gro for the heart! God's Word that has been hidden deep within me has marked and transformed my life in four distinct ways.

Reasoning – Think Like Jesus

My **reasoning** has been transformed in such a way that I have begun to **think** more **like Jesus**. This transformation is the result of first, setting my mind on the truth of scripture rather than the relative truth of the world. Then I began to practice what I call "Biting my brain."

My mom always said, "Bite your tongue!" whenever I was tempted to say something critical about someone else. I used this same idea by utilizing God's Word as teeth to bite a lie whenever it entered my mind. Instead of believing the lie, I would instead choose to believe God's truth. Over time I realized that my old "garbage" thoughts were transformed and I began to take hold of God's Word above the enemies lies.

> *"Do not conform any longer to the pattern of the world, but be transformed by the renewing of your minds, then you will be able to test and approve what God's will is, his good, pleasing, and perfect will." (Romans 12:2)*

Responses – Act Like Jesus

Secondly, my **responses** or the way I reacted to difficult circumstances in my daily life started to change. I began to **act like Jesus** rather than like the world. Instead of reacting with fear, doubt, or anger, I was able to recall scripture and reached out to God and His Word for courage, hope, and peace, especially when I found myself in an overwhelming circumstance.

> *"I have told you these things so that in me you may have peace. In this world you will have trouble. But take heart! I have overcome the world." (John 16:33)*

Relationships – Love Like Jesus

As my reasoning and my responses were changed, so were my **relationships.** Because I was becoming a changed person, transformation had to occur there as well. I began to **love like Jesus!** To love like Christ means that you give grace to the difficult people in your life, blessings to friends and enemies, and words of truth to those in need.

> *"To sum up, let all be harmonious, sympathetic, brotherly, kindhearted, and humble in spirit; not returning evil for evil or insult for insult, but giving a blessing instead. For you were called for this very purpose that you might inherit a blessing." (1 Peter 3:8-9, NASB)*

Shortly after memorizing this verse, we moved into a new condo where we encountered our very unpleasant next-door neighbor. My husband and I sought to live out the truth of this verse by finding ways to bless our neighbor whenever we came face to face with him, by first saying to ourselves, "Let's make him smile!" Much to our amazement, we usually did just that!

In fact we grew to genuinely love our neighbor by first choosing to obey the truth of God's Word! We began to love like Jesus. Relating with others who are grieving, who need advice, or who are just in need of a little encouragement comes with ease now that the Word is stored up in my mind. I used to try to give words of comfort or encouragement, but they seemed empty and without much power. Now sharing the Word comes naturally when relating with others and I can see how much power God's Word has to give hope, help, and healing.

Reputation – Look Like Jesus

As God's Word began to change the way I reasoned, responded and loved, people began to notice. The fourth distinct transformation that occurred was to my **reputation**. I developed a reputation for always having a scripture to share or to pray in times of need. People lovingly referred to me as their concordance when they needed to find out where a certain verse was found. Whenever anyone asks me about memorizing scripture I cannot help but passionately share with them how it is the one habit in my life that has brought my greatest life transformation – to **look like Jesus**!

> *"Your words were found and I ate them. Your words became for me a joy and the delight of my heart; for I have been called by Your name O Lord God of Hosts."*
> *(Jeremiah 15:16, NASB)*

When God's Word is stored up in your heart, the Holy Spirit will remind you of the Word with timely precision. Once I discovered 1 Peter 4:11, "If one speaks he should do it as one speaking the very words of God," I realized that hiding God's Word in my heart had equipped me to be a speaker and teacher who would literally speak the very words of God.

One Saturday evening, as I was soaking in the bathtub, preparing to pamper myself with a pedicure and manicure, I got a call from my Sunday morning Bible study teacher. She was stranded in an airport due to bad weather and asked if I would be able to teach her class the next day. I laughed out loud and asked if she were serious! You see, our class had about 400 in attendance each week and the thought of me standing before such a large class with a hastily prepared lesson made my heart race.

Needless to say, I was a bit surprised and totally unprepared to teach a lesson, or so I thought. After the initial shock, I asked what verse she was planning to teach. She had been teaching through the book of 1 Peter and to my amazement, the verse she gave me to teach a lesson on just happened to be one I had hidden in my heart.

> *"But you are a chosen people, a royal priesthood, a holy nation, a people belonging to God, that you may declare the praises of him who called you out of darkness into his wonderful light." (1 Peter 2:9)*

I agreed to teach and since it was so late, I prayed, asking the Lord to give me a lesson in the morning. Then I went to bed. The Lord woke me up with an outline based on the scripture and reminded me of other memory verses that supported each point. I had an outline and a handout by class time that morning. That scripture had marked my life many years before, preparing me for the day I would be called on to teach a lesson of how God marks our lives as chosen, royal, and belonging to Him. I shall never forget that day and how He chose to use me to declare His praises!

In Waylon Moore's book *Living God's Word*, Moore tells how the life of Miss Jones, a missionary to China, was dramatically impacted by a verse of scripture, which had been given to her by her friend, Dawson Trotman.

> *Dawson Trotman escorted Miss Jones to the ship that would take her back to the mission field. He prayed for her and shared a scripture with her. Shortly after arriving in China, a civil war broke out and the communists took over the government. This in turn brought about great persecution of all Christians, especially missionaries. Many were killed and some even took their own lives in the face of such great suffering. Miss Jones, however, made it out of China and back to the United States, where she went immediately to visit Mr. Trotman. Upon arriving in his office she explained all that she had witnessed and experienced at the hands of the communists and wanted to thank him for sharing with her the verse of scripture before she departed. She told Mr. Trotman, "I memorized it while traveling across the Pacific. God used it powerfully, shielding me from suicide. Thank you. That verse saved my life."* [7]

I want to be a "Dawson Trotman" to someone in my life. Can you imagine the blessing of hearing someone say to you: "Thank you for sharing that scripture with me, it saved my ... marriage, my relationship with my children, or even ... my life?" This can be said to anyone who chooses to allow God's Word to make its mark on his or her life.

I do not ever want to forget how God's Word has marked my life. This is why I write these things down in my journal so that I shall never forget.

I have a journal in which I write down my quiet time insights, prayers, sermon notes, Bible study notes, and notes on how God's Word is working in my life. It is a history of my relationship with God and others and a reminder of the marks God's Word has made on my life. It is also a way to strengthen or encourage myself in the Lord.

> *"But David strengthened himself in the Lord His God."*
> *(1 Samuel 30:6b, NASB)*

Sometimes my spiritual journey leads me to lonely times when I can't count on others to point out what God is doing in my life, so I use my journal as a pointing finger to show me and remind me that I am a woman marked by the Word.

Taking it to Heart

"For nothing is hidden except
to be revealed; nor has anything
been secret but that it should
come to light."

Mark 4:22 - NASB

Day One: Pressing On!

1. Pray, asking God to prove this scripture in your life in a very practical way. Ask Him to reveal new insights into this verse.

2. Use the meditation process to cement this verse in your mind.

3. Take the spiral with you wherever you go today and review the verse as you travel in your car, brush your teeth, do laundry, wait in line, before you eat each meal, and before going to sleep tonight.

4. Begin making a list of how specific scripture verses have marked your life.

5. Review verses from the past weeks.

Days Two–Seven: Living Intentionally!

1. Connect with your accountability partner and share your new verse.

2. Pray the verse for yourself and others.

3. Share the verse with someone each day as an encouragement, in an email, a telephone conversation, or a note.

4. Be alert to opportunities to prove the verse in your life.

5. Challenge yourself and see if you can talk to yourself or someone else for at least five minutes about the verse you are memorizing this week. Talk about its meaning, ways to apply it to your life, and any other insights you may have received from meditating on it.

"SO I WILL ALWAYS REMIND YOU OF THESE THINGS, EVEN THOUGH YOU KNOW THEM AND ARE FIRMLY ESTABLISHED IN THE TRUTH YOU NOW HAVE. I THINK IT IS RIGHT TO REFRESH YOUR MEMORY AS LONG AS I LIVE IN THE TENT OF THIS BODY."

2 Peter 1:12-13

Chapter Five

MOMENTUM:
MAINTAINING YOUR GRIP
ON THE WORD

EATING ONE POTATO chip has never been easy for me! If I dare open a bag of potato chips, the bottom of the bag becomes my destined finish line. I cannot just eat one chip, and I have learned that I cannot stop eating God's Word. Once I tasted the Word and found such rich flavor, I cannot stop eating it (1 Peter 2:3). People ask me often how I have continued to memorize scripture over the years and the answer is, "I started and I can't quit."

This is the last step in getting a grip on God's Word, and it may well be the key to developing a lifestyle of scripture memory.

When clinching your fingers together in a fist, the thumb is the part that helps you maintain your grip. Momentum is not just maintenance or maintaining the status quo, but it is about maintaining and strengthening your grip on the Word throughout a lifetime. Many people begin well enough, but there seems to only be a few who end well.

On the last night of a summer discipleship training program, the leader of the group stood before us and cautioned us to finish well by making this statement, "Some of you will not be walking with God ten years from now."

I shall never forget his words that still challenge me to maintain my grip on the spiritual disciplines I started practicing that summer over thirty years ago. These are the things that I do that help me stay on this lifetime journey of taking the Word to heart:

Review often what God has done

I began prayer journaling over twenty years ago and since memorizing scripture, I have begun to keep a record of what God has done in my heart and life through his memorized Word.

> *"For this very reason we must pay closer attention to what we have heard lest we drift away from it." (Hebrews 2:1, NASB)*

Therefore, keep a journal that you write in often, recording what God has shown you through His Word and how He has proved His Word in your life. Recently I have been taking the time to read over my last completed journal, and using a marker, I highlight the times God has spoken or moved in my life clearly through those scriptures hidden in my heart. So go back occasionally and read through your journal as a reminder of what He has done in your life and as a safeguard to keep you from drifting away from it.

Intentionally pursue a disciplined life

I no longer have to make a daily decision whether or not I am going to memorize scripture. It is a done deal. I intentionally make it a part of my daily routine.

> *"But you, man of God, flee from all of this and pursue righteousness, godliness, faith, love, endurance and gentleness." (1 Timothy 6:11)*

We do only those things that we intend on doing! Go after a life of hiding God's Word in your heart. It is an act of the will and not done out of emotion. You just do it!

Develop spiritual fervor

A few years ago, I began to write out in my prayer journal daily this prayer: "Lord, give me a passion for Your Word, Your ways, Your ministry, and Your will." It is amazing how God answers such prayers!

> *"Never be lacking in zeal, but keep your spiritual fervor, serving the Lord." (Romans 12:11)*

Fervor is passion and enthusiasm sparked by purpose. Spiritual fervor and a passion to hide God's Word in my heart developed as I followed these principles:

Commit to show up daily

Being faithfully committed to anything is rare in our culture. It is so rare that those who faithfully show up are rewarded greatly. Such was the case with baseball great Cal Ripken when he received the longest standing ovation in a baseball stadium and a new car just for playing in the most consecutive professional baseball games in history. However, when you show up daily to spend time with the Lord, you can be assured of receiving a crown that will never fade away!

"And when the Chief Shepherd appears, you will receive the crown of glory that will never fade away." (1 Peter 5:4).

A godly man who influenced my walk with Christ once said, "Nancy, keep standing at the shore and the tide will surely come in." We all go through dry times in our relationship with Christ and it is in those times that we must develop the discipline of standing at the shore, even when we don't see the tide coming. It is a long-term investment that may not show a lot of profit at first, but over time you will reap a harvest of righteousness and peace.

Do the right thing; and when you slip up, do the next right thing!

They say that if the horse bucks you off, it is best to get back on it! When your well-intended plans do not work out, go back to the drawing board and see where your plan failed. Pick up where you left off, doing the next right thing.

"You were running a good race. Who cut in on you and kept your from obeying the truth?" (Galatians 5:7)

Avoid these "Word-chokers!"

The Lord warned us that if we are not on our guard, worries, deceitfulness of wealth, and desires for other things will choke out the truth of His Word.

> *"But the worries of this life, the deceitfulness of wealth and the desires for other things come in and choke the word, making it unfruitful." (Mark 4:19)*

Worries of this life

The worries of this life can overwhelm us and before we know it, we are dried out spiritually. When my children were teenagers, there was always a fire to put out. I was often called in to help with a project the night before it was due, give counsel concerning a friend's hurt feelings, or coordinate the snacks for the basketball season. I have learned over the years that I must carve out the time to refill my mind with the Word daily before tackling the worries of this life. All these worries in life can begin to choke out the good that God is doing with His Word in our hearts. The Word becomes watered down. Instead choose to think on the true, noble, right, lovely, admirable, excellent, and praiseworthy things, and then the Word will once again be full strength in your life! (Philippians 4:8)

Deceitfulness of wealth

Our lives can become so overwhelmed by the pursuit of more money, more education, more friends, and more status that our storehouse of heavenly things sits in the shadow of our storehouse of earthly things. Recently we moved from a 2400-square foot home with a two-car garage to a 1300-square foot, two-bedroom condominium with no garage. We began to realize how attached to "things" we had become. What once appeared to us as boxes of wealth became boxes of junk! I looked at each box and thought to myself, "How deceived I was to fill up that box with things for which I now have no room or time!"

> "Do not store up for yourselves treasures on earth where moths and rust destroy, and where thieves break in and steal. But store up for yourselves treasures in heaven, where moth and rust do not destroy, and where thieves do not break in and steal. For where your treasure is, there your heart will be also." (Matthew 6:19-21)

You see, when we store up earthly treasures to excess, it only crowds out heavenly treasures, which are timeless and endless treasures given by God for our good and for His pleasure.

Desires for "other things"

Saying no to good things is hard for me. As a child of an alcoholic, I learned to be a people-pleaser in order to survive in a chaotic home. I didn't want to rock the boat so I developed a pattern of trying to please others. Because of this, I find that I take on too many "other things" in my life that tend to crowd out the "best things." Titus 2:11–12 is a scripture hidden in my heart which instructs me to say no to "ungodliness and worldly desires and to live sensibly, righteously, and godly in the present age." (NASB) Now I test these other things that want to choke out truth by asking myself, "Is the thing sensible, righteous and godly?" If it is, then I say "yes," and if it is not, I say "no!"

Begin Again Each Time I Falter

When I give in to the Word-chokers and allow them to make my life fruitless, I become miserable. I have learned that until the pain of staying the same becomes greater than the pain of change, I will remain fruitless. But when that fruitless pain becomes great, I give way to change and begin again on the journey.

These are the steps I take to begin again:

Repent and return to God

> *"Repent then and turn to God, so that your sins may be wiped out, that times of refreshing may come from the Lord" (Acts 3:19).*

For a fresh start, admit to God and yourself that you have become lax or have failed to keep your commitment. Ask for forgiveness and a fresh start. Whenever we get honest with God and share our heart's desire with Him, He is faithful to forgive. He is much like that special friend who no matter how often or seldom you see them, you just take up where you left off, as if no time had passed. Hebrews 12:15 is a truth that set me free from this all-or-nothing thinking. It says, "See to it that no one misses the grace of God …" When I first memorized that verse, I focused on giving grace to others when they hurt me or made mistakes. I have finally realized that I am a part of that "no one." I am learning to accept God's grace that says, "Nancy, you didn't hide my Word in your heart this week, and that is okay, just begin again today." I extend myself grace when I do not keep up with the commitment of a weekly verse. I figure that God wants me to spend an extra week or two on some verses or that I need an extra week to just review the verses I already stored in my heart.

Get up!

Don't allow the enemy to fill your mind with lies such as "I can't" and "give up!" Instead, listen to this truth:

> "Do not gloat over me, my enemy! Though I have fallen, I will rise. Though I sit in darkness the Lord will be my light." (Micah 7:8)

Tell the enemy that you may have fallen down in your commitment, but that by the grace of God you are getting back up!

Don't look back!

Don't dwell on unmet goals or feelings of failure. Instead, set your sights on the path, taking the next step forward (Philippians 3:12–16). Start where you are and ask God for a new verse and to do something new in your life (Isaiah 43:18–19). After being on my scripture memory journey for several years I memorized:

> "Teach us to number our days aright, that we may gain a heart of wisdom." (Psalm 90:12)

This came to mind as our pastor was teaching through the book of Nehemiah and gave us this challenge: "What could God rebuild in your life if you gave Him fifty-two days?" This challenge was based on the number of days it took the men to rebuild the wall of Jerusalem.

"So the wall was completed on the twenty-fifth of Elul, in fifty-two days. When all the enemies heard about this, all the surrounding nations were afraid and lost their self-confidence, because they realized that this work had been done with the help of our God" (Nehemiah 6:15,16)

As I prayed about what God would have me do, I took the truth of numbering my days in Psalm 90:12 and combined the idea of asking God to rebuild or build something in my life every fifty-two days. I took my calendar and divided the 365 days of the year into seven fifty-two day segments with one day left over. I started my fifty-two day segment by praying over what goals the Lord would have me set for the next fifty-two days. Then I numbered that day 1, the next day 2, and so on until I came to the fifty-second day. On that last day I read through the last fifty-two days of my journal noting all God had done in my life as I memorized, meditated and mobilized His Word. This is a habit I continue to practice and it has helped me to stay focused on my present tasks rather than looking back in regret at what I failed to accomplish.

Keep Going!

Recently I pulled into a one-way entrance to our church parking lot. As I drove through the narrow entrance, I realized that a huge truck blocked me in. It was parked at an angle, blocking me from entering the parking lot. I could not go backwards because it led back into the path of the freeway access road. I was stuck! I had about three minutes to get to a meeting, so I called several people that I knew were inside the church building to seek help. Finally, the driver of the truck appeared and moved his truck, freeing me to move forward and park. That was a great reminder to me of how we do allow those "chokers" in our lives to be roadblocks to our spiritual growth. It also showed me that all I needed to do was call for help and eventually it came— giving me power to move ahead.

Once You are Back on the Road to Growth, Keep Moving Forward

You never stand still spiritually. You are either going forward or backward!

> "Let us not grow weary in doing good, for at the proper time you will reap a harvest if you do not give up."
> (Galatians 6:9)

So get up and keep going in your pursuit of God's truth. God is a creative God who is actively pursuing fellowship with us. So, it makes sense to seek out creative ways to make the scripture memory journey more practical and powerful.

One creative way for me to maintain this spiritual momentum has been to ask God for a word each year. My friend, Pat, would always talk about how God had given her a word each year. I wanted what Pat had, so I asked God to give me a word. This was over ten years ago and God has been faithful to give me a new word to focus on each year. I began asking God in the summer to show me a word that He wants me to grow in.

For example the first year God gave me two words: obey and finish. I kept seeing these words through scripture, hearing them in sermons, and reading them in devotional books. It was also the year I decided I needed to obediently write this book. So I began memorizing scriptures about obedience or finishing. Those verses were the fuel God supplied me with to complete writing the first edition of this book.

Since that first year of asking God for a word, He has supplied me with such words as faithful, strength, courage, and abide. Every year I look forward with great excitement to see what word God will lead me to focus on and learn from. (See Appendix for A Year's Supply of Momentum Memory Verses.)

Follow God's Prompting to Pass It On

When you become passionate about something, you can't help but share it with those around you. The power of God's Word in your life can be multiplied when you are obedient to share with others these words of life, hope, and help. Success in your life breeds success in others. Each time I am asked to teach an individual or present a seminar to a group about how to get a grip on God's Word, I can't start talking quickly enough! The more opportunities I have to share my story or simply share a scripture with someone who is discouraged the more committed I become to a lifetime of hiding God's Word in my heart.

> *"Let the Word of Christ dwell in you richly as you teach and admonish one another with all wisdom and as you sing psalms, hymns and spiritual songs with gratitude in your hearts to God." (Colossians 3:16)*

After a few years of teaching people how to memorize scripture, I was constantly being asked, "Nancy, do you have a book that explains further what you have just taught?" This book is the result of a God-given desire to share with others this incredible habit that will transform a life.

During the first year of my personal scripture memory journey, when I committed to the Lord to memorize one scripture verse a week for fifty-two weeks, I learned to persevere through challenges. My goal was to be able to quote all fifty-two verses at the end of the year and therefore, my goal was my motivation. It was the vision that I kept before me each week as I began learning a new verse.

Bill Parcels, the former head coach of the Dallas Cowboys, once said, "This year will bring many challenges, but it will not lessen the vision." That was my mindset as I journeyed that first year of scripture memorization and it is the key to consistency in disciplining your life spiritually or physically.

All-or-nothing thinking is common among those who are trying to discipline themselves for the purpose of godliness or for the purpose physical fitness. We begin a diet or workout plan and at the first hint of trouble we quit, telling ourselves that we will begin next week. Unfortunately, one week becomes one month, and before we know it we are desperately in a never-ending yo-yo cycle of weight loss and weight gain, never reaching that goal we had envisioned. We turn in to "should've, could've, and would've" people, always making excuses and living in regret.

The same is true in our spiritual discipline, and the enemy is having a celebration at our expense, for he is keeping us from enjoying all that we have as children of the King.

> "But I am afraid that, as the serpent deceived Eve by his craftiness, your minds will be led astray from the simplicity and purity of devotion to Christ." (2 Corinthians 11:3)

Don't be deceived, but simply memorize, meditate, and mobilize the Word in your life. Then you will be marked by pure devotion to Christ as you keep the vision of your goal of taking the Word to heart before you.

A Closing Reminder

As you begin this journey of scripture memorization, remember that each part of gripping the Word builds a tighter grasp on it.

Memorize:
Manned with a Purpose and a Plan

God created the hand with five fingers that work together to open a door, pick up a glass of water, hold a fork, or do many other everyday tasks. A pinky finger doesn't have the strength to open a door on its own, but when using all the fingers together it opens easily. In the same way, to begin strengthening your grip on God's Word you must begin with memorizing it. The discipline of **memorizing** is essential, just as the **pinky** is essential to gripping a hand, but it is just the beginning.

Meditate:
Chew on the Word and Consider its Meaning

The second part of gripping the Word, **meditate**, can be compared to the **ring finger** of a hand. I wear my college class ring on my ring finger, which symbolizes the time and commitment it took to earn my degree. Meditating on God's Word takes time, but yields the accomplishment of a deeper knowledge of scripture and God's character.

Mobilize:
Applying the Word to Your Life

Gaining knowledge through meditating on the memorized Word can lead to spiritual pride unless one does what it says or mobilizes its truths into their life.

"Knowledge puffs up, but love builds up." (1 Corinthians 8:1b)

Therefore, the third essential step in the process of taking His Word to heart is learning to apply your knowledge of scripture to real-life circumstances or **mobilize** the Word true in your life. This helps you to grow stronger in your walk with Christ, so mobilizing God's Word can be symbolized by our **third finger** because it is the tallest and the strongest part of the grip.

Marked:
Being Transformed by the Word

When you mobilize scripture in your life you will be forever **marked** by God in such dramatic ways that people will begin to notice your transformation. The marked process compares to your **pointer finger** because others begin to take notice and point out the ways you have begun to think, act, love and look more like Jesus.

Momentum:
Maintaining Your Grip on the Word

Lastly, **the thumb** holds the other four fingers of the grip together, just as practicing spiritual **momentum** will allow you to grip tightly God's Word for a lifetime and finish your journey with a "thumbs up" and a crown that will never fade away.

> *"And when the Chief Shepherd appears, you will receive the crown of glory that will never fade away." (1 Peter 5:4)*

God's Word, once rooted in your heart, will bring you joy beyond measure. It will give you knowledge of your Creator, a willing and obedient heart, and a deeper trust in the one who loves you like no other.

Taking it to Heart

"Never be lacking in zeal,
but keep your spiritual fervor,
serving the Lord."

Romans 12:11

Day One: Pressing On!

1. Keep a list of scriptures to memorize

   - Choose a variety of topics and authors to stay balanced in your knowledge.

   - Choose verses and passages that relate to you and your current life circumstances.

   - Some suggested verses and passages:

     - Philippians 2 (humility)
     - Psalm 100 (praise)
     - Isaiah 55 (the Word)
     - 2 Corinthians 4 (ministry)
     - A Year's Supply of Memory Verses (see Appendix)

Day Two and Forward: Living Intentionally!

1. Develop a plan for review that works for you!

_____

_____

_____

_____

_____

_____

_____

_____

_____

2. Avoid Word-chokers—list those that are most tempting to you and ask God's help in pursuing a godly lifestyle.

_____

_____

_____

_____

_____

_____

_____

_____

_____

3. Begin again each time you fall:

- Repent

- Get up

- Don't look back – Try numbering your days, committing your plans to the Lord one day at a time. What would you like God to rebuild in your life over the next 52 days?

- Keep going – Ask God to give you a word to focus on for a year. Look up verses that use that word and begin memorizing, meditating on them, and mobilizing them in your life. Write down in your journal ways that word marks your life.

Appendix

A YEAR'S SUPPLY
OF MEMORY VERSES

Scripture Memorization

1. Jeremiah 15:16
2. Psalm 1:2–3
3. Psalm 119:30
4. Deuteronomy 30:14
5. Hebrews 2:1
6. Colossians 3:16
7. Matthew 6:19–21

Overcoming Temptation

1. Psalm 119:11
2. 1 Corinthians 10:13
3. Titus 2:11–12
4. Psalm 119:37
5. Micah 7:7–8
6. Psalm 19:13
7. 2 Corinthians 10:4
8. Psalm 18:28–29

Renewing and Preparing the Mind

1. Romans 12:2
2. Colossians 3:1–2
3. Psalm 51:12
4. 1 Peter 1:13
5. 2 Corinthians 4:16
6. Psalm 94:19
7. 2 Corinthians 10:5

Receiving Direction and Guidance

1. Micah 6:8
2. Psalm 90:12
3. Psalm 143:8
4. John 14:26
5. John 16:33
6. Isaiah 55:11
7. Psalm 119:105

Developing Godly Character

1. 2 Peter 1:4
2. 2 Corinthians 4:7
3. Luke 6:45
4. Philippians 2:12–13
5. Hebrews 12:11
6. 2 Corinthians 1:20
7. Proverbs 15:15

Establishing Prayer Life

1. John 15:7
2. Matthew 21:22
3. Psalm 57:2
4. Psalm 37:4
5. 1 Peter 4:7
6. Colossians 1:9–10
7. Ephesians 3:20

Sharing with Others

1. Zephaniah 3:17
2. Psalm 3:3
3. Isaiah 50:4
4. Matthew 11:28–30
5. Romans 5:8
6. Romans 3:22–24
7. Romans 6:23
8. Ephesians 2:8-9
9. Ephesians 2:10

A Year's Supply of
Momentum Memory Verses

Faithful

1. Matthew 25:21
2. Proverbs 24:30-34
3. Hosea 6:3
4. 1 Corinthians 1:9
5. Proverbs 11:6
6. Romans 12:12
7. Hebrews 10:23

Strength

1. Psalm 18:1-3
2. Psalm 138:3
3. 2 Timothy 2:1
4. 2 Corinthians 12:9-10
5. Ephesians 1:17-20
6. 2 Thessalonians 2:16-17
7. Isaiah 41:9-10
8. Deuteronomy 6:5

Courage

1. Deuteronomy 31:6
2. Psalm 27:13–14
3. Matthew 14:27
4. John 16:33
5. Acts 4:13
6. Joshua 1:7
7. 1 Corinthians 16:13

Gospel

1. 2 Corinthians 5:20-21
2. Romans 1:16
3. Romans 10:9
4. 1 Peter 3:15
5. Acts 4:12
6. Colossians 1:13-14
7. Ephesians 2:4-5
8. Acts 20:24

New

1. Romans 6:4
2. 2 Corinthians 5:17
3. Psalm 96:1-2
4. Isaiah 42:8-9
5. Ezekiel 36:26
6. Mark 2:21-22
7. Isaiah 43:18-19

Obey

1. Psalm 119:4-5
2. Isaiah 50:10
3. Philippians 2:12-13
4. Deuteronomy 30:14
5. Deuteronomy 32:46-47
6. John 15:10
7. John 14:21

Love

1. 1 John 3:1
2. Romans 8:38-39
3. 1 Corinthians 13: 4-7
4. Deuteronomy 33:12
5. Matthew 6:19-21
6. Matthew 22:37-40
7. Lamentations 3:21-23
8. John 13:34-35

Acknowledgments

I want to thank . . .

My Lord Jesus Christ for His powerful Word that continues to transform my life.

My husband and best friend, William, for his constant encouragement.

My children, Will and Sarah for living out the truth of 3 John 4: "I have no greater joy than to hear that my children are walking in the truth."

Pat Lewis for her early editing and for cheering me on to the finish line.

Erin Robison, Erin Robinson Coaching, for encouraging me to develop a plan for reaching my goal.

Dianna Tyrrell for editing this new and improved edition.

James Woosley of Free Agent Press, for guidance and co-laboring with me in the publishing process.

My accountability partners, Vicky Wright, Diane Bagby, Denise Munton, Carolyn O'Neal, and Sue Hurst for their support and prayers.

All those who have read my book or attended one of my scripture memory classes and are proving His Word true in their lives.

About the Author

NANCY TAYLOR is a teacher, speaker and mentor to young women. She has a passion for sharing throughout the world the transforming power of God's memorized Word. She coordinates a mentoring ministry at Houston's First Baptist Church, Houston, Texas where her husband William serves as the Missions Pastor.

Notes

Getting to Know God and His Word

Chapter One – Memorize: Manned with a Purpose and a Plan

1. Cynthia Heald, *Becoming a Woman of Excellence* (Colorado Springs: Nav- Press, 2005), p. 77.

2. John Maxwell, *Leadership Wired* (InJoy Inc, April 2002, Vol. 5, Issue 7)

Chapter Two – Meditate: Chew On the Word and Consider its Meaning

3. Wikipedia , the free encyclopedia

4. Waylon B. Moore, *Living God's Word* (Nashville: Life-Way Press, 1997) p.50.

Developing a Heart of Obedience

5. Cynthia Heald, *Becoming a Woman of Excellence* (Colorado Springs: Nav- Press 2005) p. 39

Chapter Three – Mobilize: Applying the Word to Your Life

6. Neil Anderson, *Daily in Christ* (Eugene, OR: Harvest House Publishers) January 1 entry.

Living a Life of Trust

Chapter Four – Mark: Being Transformed by the Word

7. Waylon B. Moore, *Living God's Word* (Nashville: Life-Way Press, 1997) p.50.

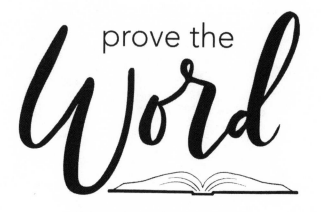

provetheword.org